Outdoor Cooking from Tide's Table

Ross & Willa Mavis

Outdoor Cooking *from*

Tide's Table

GOOSE LANE

Edited by Jennifer Lambert.
Cover photography by Brian Atkinson. Art direction by Julie Scriver.
Book design by Julie Scriver.
Printed in Canada by Transcontinental.
10 9 8 7 6 5 4 3 2 1

Canadian Cataloguing in Publication Data

Mavis, Ross, 1941-
Outdoor cooking from Tide's Table

Includes index.
ISBN 0-86492-296-5

1. Outdoor cookery.   2. Barbecue cookery.
I. Mavis, Willa, 1945-   II. Title
TX823.M39 2000   641.5'78   C00-900150-6

Published with the financial support of the Government of Canada through
the Book Publishing Industry Development Program and the New Brunswick
Department of Economic Development, Tourism and Culture.

Goose Lane Editions
469 King Street
Fredericton, New Brunswick
CANADA E3B 1E5

CONTENTS

INTRODUCTION

Ross's Version

I'll never forget my first barbecue or the little manual that came with it. On the inside cover, a cartoon entitled "How It All Began" illustrates the evolution of barbecuing. The first panel shows a caveman holding a slab of meat on a stick over an open fire. Smoke swirls around him and his family as they sit in front of their cave, waiting and watching hopefully. The next panel depicts a Victorian woman stirring a large cauldron hanging over the hearth. This is followed by a rather grim-faced cook stoking a wood-burning stove. Next we see a fifties-style housewife daintily attending a pot on her thoroughly modern electric range. The final panel is almost identical to the first. It shows a man holding a steak on a fork over a flaming barbecue. Smoke swirls around him and his family as they sit on their deck, waiting and watching hopefully.

The cartoon says it all. Haute cuisine has come full circle, back to the days of cave culture. Smoke is once more in the air. Can you smell it? Not the smoke of fashionable cigars, but the kind that conjures up images of plundering, pillaging, and prehistoric cookouts. You know the smell I mean — that uncertain sweet, sooty aroma that makes you wonder if it's the meat or your sleeve that's burning.

It's an intriguing time, when sophisticated and expensive kitchens and cooking paraphernalia are spurned for the call of the open flame. Barbecuing was originally a "black art," and it remains that way for many people today. Witness the burnt offerings from many backyard charcoal altars, which are consumed with such relish. Never mind the second- or third-degree burns we cheerfully risk to slather barbecue sauce on steak for the family. Our ancestors faced double the challenge. First they had to fell the savage beast and hope it landed close to the fire. A poorly launched spear or rock might force the entire community to move several miles in order to chow down. Now we have it easy — portable charcoal or propane grills ended the need for the mastodon to come to Mohammed. Cookers of all shapes and sizes grace our patios and decks, just waiting for a massive slab of protein to be slapped onto their smoking grills. Ah, the very thought of it brings out the beast in me.

Concerns about cholesterol and carcinogens are cast to the wind with the striking of a match to briquettes, of flint to propane. And who among us won't risk a sunburn to step outside in the midday sun to grill a juicy steak or, for that matter, chilblains in deep winter when the hunger for a hamburger strikes?

Barbecuing allows men, in particular, to feel that we can vanquish mighty foes and provide food for our families. We have wrestled the beast to the ground, or at least battled rush-hour traffic to get to the supermarket sirloin. We spend countless hours perfecting the secret sauce or marinade that will bring honour to our household. We risk peril to life and limb while ministering to the prime ribs sizzling over a captive volcano on the deck.

This is indeed stuff of which legends are made. But why is it that barbecuing is primarily the domain of men? History tells us that only one woman of note was involved in an outdoor cookout. And while no one would want to suffer like Joan of Arc, there must be a greater reason why women have chosen to relinquish our guts-and-glory gatherings around the communal fire.

Surely it couldn't be the slight inconvenience of cleaning up a greasy crematorium like the interior of a barbecue. I'm sure it wouldn't have anything to do with the laundry stains caused by sputtering steak sauce. Nor would the clouds of grimy smoke and the urge to utter profanities at frequent flare-ups be reasons for women to reject their rightful place in this great outdoor adventure. Let me leave these steaks on the grill, while I ask my wife why this horrendous injustice has occurred. . . . Let's see now. . . . I think she's on the other side of the deck . . . out of the wind . . . getting the sun . . . reclining on the chaise longue with an iced tea and a best-seller. . . .

— *Ross Mavis*

Willa's Version

Ross has taken the usual male attitude towards barbecuing, hasn't he? While he's slaving over a hot grill, I'm relaxing in the shade with a cool drink. Read on.

My barbecuing career began about 34 years ago, using a round, red tin affair filled with charcoal and started by pouring copious amounts of starter fluid (i.e., kerosene) over the coals, standing back, and throwing in a lighted match. This smelly, foul stuff added an oily flavour to whatever was being cooked, no matter how long you waited for the coals to burn down. The meat — generally large, one-pound-per-person steaks — was burnt on the outside and raw in the middle. But I was very young and thought it was gourmet fare. After all, my dad never cooked, indoors or out, so this was pretty sophisticated stuff.

Slowly, things evolved. We still used charcoal, but the grills improved. They could be raised and lowered, therefore improving our chances of controlling the temperature. The meat burned less, and we purchased an electric prong that fit nicely under the briquettes to light them slowly without the use of petrochemicals. However, there was no spontaneous cooking. Barbecues still had to be planned. Tempers rose when charcoal ran out or was found in a soggy bag, and the stores were closed on Sunday. We weren't having a lot of fun.

Finally, gas barbecues arrived at the local hardware store. Yes, they were expensive. But quick arithmetic proved that the savings outweighed the cost of the tank and propane. And anyway, they were trendy and quick. Now we could do simple things, like barbecued hot dogs for lunch, just because we wanted to. No more planning.

I began cooking on a gas range when I was a young bride of 20. I loved it right from the start, so moving to a gas barbecue was very easy. My son was constantly bringing friends home for lunch, and for five straight years, I fed several neighbourhood boys a diet of hot dogs and Kool-Aid. I was very popular with the boys and with their mothers, who were able to lie on their chaise longues reading the latest Harold Robbins novel while I entertained their kids.

From hot dogs and hamburgers, I graduated to steaks, chops, fish, and vegetables. I discovered the wonders of cooking with foil (and the joy of no pots to clean). I'm an outdoor person, so the barbecue was made for me. Camp stove cooking was also a big part of my early years. In addition to tenting, we sailed, cooking on a two-burner gas stove for weeks at a time. On two occasions we lived on a sailboat for a year, and I became adept at cooking somewhat-gourmet meals on small gas tops. And living in the country, we often had power failures. The portable camping stove was always nearby, and complete dinners of stews, soups, meat, and vegetables still found their way to our dinner table.

When Ross and I moved to Toronto, our tiny house had no air conditioning. I walked from room to room carrying a portable fan and was unable to do anything on hot, humid days. We solved the problem of eating by having not only a gas barbecue in our beautiful backyard, but also a gas camp stove. We quite literally lived outdoors during the long summer days and evenings, but we continued to eat in "the style to which we had become accustomed." Each meal consisted of a meat or fish dish, accompanied by at least four fresh vegetables and maybe a quick dessert. Entertaining was no problem. We simply added an extra setting or two to our round patio table and threw another rib on the grill.

I said in our first cookbook, *Tide's Table: Maritime Cooking from Inn on the Cove*, that I married Ross for his ribs. Well, these are the ribs I was referring to. He would parboil them in our pressure cooker on the camp stove (saving the broth for a great soup base) while I made a barbecue sauce and prepared the veggies. The ribs went on the grill just long enough to brown them, and we had no problem convincing people to stay to dinner.

Like everything that Ross and I do, we barbecue together. So pshaw, Ross, the barbecue is no more your exclusive domain than the kitchen sink is mine. Well, maybe that isn't the perfect analogy. Perhaps I should substitute the washing machine and dryer. No, wrong choice again. The iron and ironing board. No. Well, you know what I'm getting at, don't you? Don't let the barbecue intimidate you, man or woman. Invite your friends over, pour everyone a tall, cold drink, and just have fun. I know we do.

— *Willa Mavis*

Barbecue Basics

Barbecuing is too often approached as a form of "black art." Food cooked on a grill does not have to be black and charred to ensure that it is cooked well. The following tips, techniques, and basic procedures can make all the difference in serving succulent fare at your table.

Choosing the grill of your dreams

One of the first decisions to make when buying a barbecue is to choose the model best suited to your needs. Both size and type of fuel are important. There are three main types of barbecue on the market — charcoal, propane-fired, and electric. Each has its advantages and disadvantages. Personal preference, cooking techniques, and even local bylaws or apartment building regulations may play important roles in your decision.

Charcoal Grills

The first portable charcoal barbecues were developed centuries ago in the Orient. The hibachi, Japanese for "fire bowl," is, in fact, just that. Today, there are several types available; the Japanese hibachi cookers are small but effective, while bigger braziers provide larger grilling surfaces. All are fuelled by charcoal. The most popular type is crushed charcoal shaped into small briquettes. Natural hardwood charcoal is more expensive and less readily available. However, charcoal barbecue purists maintain that the natural product is best by far, as it contains no chemical additives to flavour or taint food.

Charcoal requires lighting and up to 45 minutes for proper coal formation prior to cooking. Over the years, petroleum-based lighting fluids, blocks, and gels have been developed, and some briquettes contain chemicals that encourage direct lighting with a match. Some people dislike the slight petroleum flavour imparted by this type of ignition. Electric briquette lighters are available but require an accessible electric outlet. A simple lighting device can be made by removing both ends of a large coffee or juice can. Punch several holes around the base of the can to allow a draft, and push several sheets of crumpled newspaper into the bottom of the can. Place the can upright inside the barbecue, on top of a few briquettes, and stack more briquettes on top of the paper. Light the paper with a match through one of the draft holes and let it burn. After about 15 or 20 minutes, carefully remove the can with a pair of pliers, letting the ignited briquettes spill into the barbecue. Once all the briquettes are burning, arrange them evenly under the grill.

Charcoal must be kept dry, and it is important to follow the manufacturer's directions concerning quantities. Usually a single layer of charcoal is sufficient for any cooking using the full grill surface. Space the briquettes or charcoal pieces apart slightly so flare-ups from dripping juices are less frequent. If the total surface of the grill is not needed, only arrange briquettes under one part to provide a cooler area where rapidly cooked food can be held. It's a mistake to use too many briquettes. Excessive heat can sometimes cause scorching, and it's a waste of money to have a hot grill long after the food is cooked.

Check the temperature by placing your palm about five inches (13 cm) over the grill. If you cannot hold it there for at least two seconds, the coals are too hot. Wait five or 10 minutes and then try again. A medium-hot heat will allow you to hold your hand over the grill for about five or six seconds. To maintain a consistent heat during cooking, occasionally knock the grey ash off the charcoal.

A word of caution: charcoal emits deadly carbon monoxide when burning and should be used only outside in a well-ventilated area. Wind can blow burning sparks from charcoal, so exercise common sense when choosing a barbecuing area. Avoid locating this type of grill close to combustible surroundings. It's also a good idea to have a bucket of water and a fire extinguisher close by for any emergency.

Electric Grills

Apartment dwellers, who may not be permitted to use charcoal or propane barbecues, can be grateful for the development of electric grills. These units are excellent for both grilled and rotisserie foods. They are fast to heat and can be used safely on a balcony with a grounded electrical outlet. Some units even allow the heating element to be moved alongside the spit, reducing the possibility of flare-ups. Although food cooked on an electric grill gives the appearance of having been barbecued, it will lack the smoky flavour that is such a large part of barbecue cooking.

Indoor electric grills are also quite effective for small crowds. Grilling indoors is not much different from cooking outside, except that smoke and cooking fumes can be a problem.

Propane Grills

Gas-fired grills are fast, convenient, and still provide the flavour of open-flame cooking. Lava or ceramic rocks or tiles encourage smoke flavour from the juices and fat drippings to permeate food. Smaller propane units with portable tanks enable you to take your barbecue on picnics, camping trips, and even sailing adventures.

Propane is an explosive gas that is heavier than air. When vented from a tank, propane will flow into and collect in low-lying areas. It is extremely important to keep this in mind when transporting tanks. Don't carry filled propane tanks in the trunk of your car; rather, secure them in the back seat with a window open to provide good ventilation. Check local regulations with your police or fire department regarding the legal transporting of propane tanks. Remember that propane tanks should be replaced and safely disposed of after 10 years.

Be sure to have an adequate supply of propane on hand before you start cooking. Nothing is worse than running out of flame before the food is cooked. The easiest way to check your tank is to lift it: A light tank indicates low or little propane. Another method that works with certain types of tanks is to dump a bucket of hot water over the tank. Once the water has run off, slide your hand down the side of the tank. If you feel a line where the tank becomes cold, this indicates the propane level. If you can't distinguish any temperature difference and the tank feels light, it's definitely time for a refill. You can also buy an inexpensive gas-level indicator. This special strip of adhesive tape with thermochromic yellow ink markings is fastened to the side of the propane tank. When water is poured down the length of the tape, it changes colour after a few seconds, and then the colder portion changes back to yellow, indicating the propane level. These indicators can be used over and over again indefinitely. Of course, to play it safe, always have a spare tank on hand. When your first tank runs out, refill it immediately and treat it as your spare.

As with other gas-fired appliances, propane grills must be used in a well-ventilated location. New units should be preheated, burning off any foreign materials or grease. Grills can be "burned off" in about 10 minutes on a high setting. Always raise the lid on a propane grill before lighting it. A closed lid can result in the barbecue filling with gas, and the starting spark could easily cause an explosion. If the burner does not light at once, turn off the controls and allow gas to disperse before trying again. Once the burner is lit, the lid can be lowered for preheating.

Lava rocks and ceramic cooking tiles covering propane burners should be turned over after every few barbecue sessions to allow any accumulated fat drippings to burn off. It's a good idea to degrease and clean the barbecue's interior at the same time. You can use hot water and detergent or a good barbecue degreasing spray. Regular cleaning will prolong the life of your grill and its burner.

Grilling techniques

General

When cooking on any grill surface, move and turn food regularly, even at low temperatures, to avoid burning. When cooking directly on the grill surface in a propane barbecue, turn off one side of the grill if food is browning too rapidly. Move food to the "off" side; the heat from the "on" side will circulate, and food will cook through without charring from direct heat. I also find that two regular concrete or clay bricks placed on the grill surface work well to elevate food above the hot grill. Skewered food in particular is best cooked above the grilling surface. Wire skewer racks can be purchased, or you can simply use the brick technique, balancing skewers between two bricks.

Stir-fries can be cooked using special perforated, enamel-coated pans or trays. These can be obtained at most stores carrying a good range of barbecue items. Even perforated pizza pans are perfect for the barbecue. The dough won't stick to the enamelled surface, and the heat gets right to the crust, browning it nicely.

Cooking with Foil

It is a good idea to keep a ready supply of aluminum foil on hand when barbecuing. Strong yet flexible, it can be folded to create a wind-break or fashioned into warming dishes for cooked foods. It can also be folded and tucked to form a temporary drip pan to catch juices and fat from grilled foods.

We are not big fans of cooking in foil on the grill. The primary reason is that the sealed foil packet keeps out the wonderful smoked and open-flame flavours for which barbecued food is famous. However, many moist vegetables and some delicate foods, such as fish, can be cooked to advantage using foil packets on the grill. When camping, aluminum foil is terrific for cooking potatoes, meat, poultry, or fish if an open fire is your only source of heat. Remember to seal aluminum foil packets well by folding seams several times. Be very careful when opening hot foil packets, as the steam can be scalding. Oven mitts are very useful, but you can also pierce packets with a fork to let the steam escape before opening.

Rotisserie Cooking

The first rotisserie I owned was battery operated. Although it worked just fine, the batteries never lasted more than one or two lengthy barbecuing sessions. And believe me, it's every bit as bad to lose rotisserie power as it is to run out of propane. Most rotisseries today are plug-in units. Rotisserie cooking offers three main advantages over regular grilling or roasting. Most important is the tender, moist flavour of meat that is basted continually throughout cooking. Rotisseried meats are also uniformly browned due to their constant turning over the heat. Best of all, once you've balanced the meat properly on the rotisserie, it requires little attention. Following a few simple steps and procedures, anyone can enjoy effortless rotisserie cooking, with wonderful results.

The weight of a roast is less important than the need for it to be of uniform thickness; this will help you to balance it on the spit, which will ensure even cooking. On the other hand, a roast that tapers at one end allows you to serve a range of meat from rare to well done. Boneless cuts of meat are best for the rotisserie and should be well trussed with butcher string or light wire; a meat thermometer is essential. It is very important to fasten meat securely to the spit before cooking, using a pair of pliers to tighten the wing nuts, as they may loosen from the heat. Estimate where the roast should be located in relation to the motor end of the spit, and secure one of the two spit forks at that place. Tighten the wing nut only by hand at this point. Then slide the meat down the spit and onto the fork. Slide the second fork onto the spit, jamming the tines into the meat, and tighten the wing nut with your fingers.

Place the spit on the barbecue to check that the meat is centred over the heat. Then remove it and hold one end in either hand to check the balance. A properly balanced spit will turn easily, ensuring even browning and cooking and helping preserve the life of your spit motor. Sometimes it is impossible to balance a roast or bird without using a spit or rotisserie weight. This invaluable accessory is a movable weight on a clamp, which helps to offset an unbalanced spit.

Once the meat is balanced, tighten the spit-fork wing nuts using pliers, and place the rotisserie onto the preheated medium-hot barbecue. Position the spit's retainer ring just inside the barbecue casing at the end opposite the motor, and tighten it using a screwdriver or pliers. This is very important, as the spit, without this retainer firmly in place, can crawl out of the motor drive assembly. (This happened to me once. Because I could hear the motor running, I didn't realize there was a problem. However, in fact the meat was standing still and burning.)

Turn on the motor, and check that the spit turns evenly and that the meat is clear of the briquettes or lava rock and any part of the barbecue. Place a drip pan in position under the meat, and add about a cup of water to prevent fat and juices from flaring up. You can fashion a drip pan out of a double thickness of aluminum foil or use a metal cake pan. Just make sure it has raised edges and is slightly larger than the circumference of the meat. Use a turkey baster to empty the pan during cooking, if necessary.

Once you are certain everything is in order, close the barbecue lid and reduce heat to low. Check the rotisserie's operation frequently during the first 15 or 20 minutes of cooking. When you are satisfied that all is working properly, you can go and reward yourself with a cold drink.

A glaze or marinade containing sugar or fruit juice should be applied to the meat only during the last five or 10 minutes of cooking to avoid burning.

Smoker Cooking

Charcoal-fired smoke kettles and small electric smokers are well suited for smoking meat, poultry, fish, and game at home. It is also possible to create smoke flavour in a covered propane barbecue by placing wood-smoke chips in a small metal pan on top of th elava rock or ceramic cooking tiles. Tins of flavoured wood-smoking chips are also available. The tin is set in the hot coals, and a hole in its top allows smoke to drift out. Different types of wood provide unique flavours. Apple, alder, hickory, mesquite, and maple are all good choices. Experiment with different combinations. Slowly cooked ham over hickory or apple-wood chips is particularly fine. Turkey with hickory is another good combination, while fish of all varieties quickly absorb any wood-smoke flavour. Thinner cuts of meat or fish absorb smoke flavour faster than thick cuts.

Brining meat or fish overnight before barbecuing over wood-smoke chips produces excellent results. (For brine recipe, see page 61.) The brine will firm up soft-fleshed fish, partially cook or preserve the flesh, and make it easy for the smoke flavour to be absorbed. Brined meat and fish should be left to air-dry for about one hour before smoking. Remember that food smoked in this manner has been flavoured, not cured, and must be handled safely. If not eaten right away, it should be covered and refrigerated.

Grilling tips

♦ Keep your grilling surface clean and ready for use.
♦ Preheat the grill with the barbecue lid closed. A closed lid will cook food faster and use less fuel.
♦ To keep food from sticking, brush grill with oil after preheating. Alternatively, another trick is to rub a freshly cut raw potato over the hot grill surface. Impale the potato on a long-handled fork to keep hands and arms well clear of flames.
♦ As grilling causes food to drip fat and juices, be sure a grease cup is installed under the bottom of the cooking unit. This should be removed and cleaned occasionally.
♦ Flare-ups from dripping grease can be minimized by spraying charcoal briquettes occasionally with water.
♦ Flare-ups in propane-fired units are best controlled with a light sprinkling of baking soda. Don't use water, as hot cast-metal surfaces can sometimes crack when they come into contact with cold water.

Grill Temperature Guide

If you are cooking over charcoal, there is an accurate way to judge the heat of your grill. Even with propane grills, you can't always rely on control settings because old, corroded burners and worn controls can result in unreliable temperatures. All grills are not created equal, so experiment with your own barbecue to decide on which temperatures are best.

Roll up your sleeves and carefully hold the palm of your hand about 5 inches (13 cm) above the grill until, the heat is too uncomfortable. Count the time it takes before you must move your hand.

Hot	2-3 seconds
Medium-Hot	3-4 seconds
Medium	4-6 seconds
Low	6-9 seconds

Meat, Fish, and Seafood Cooking Chart

BEEF				
Cut or portion — placed 4 inches (10 cm) above heat	Weight or thickness	Temperature of barbecue	Barbecue cover	Approximate cooking times
Burgers (well done)	1/2 inch (1 cm)	medium to hot	open	12-15 min
			covered	10-12 min
	3/4 inch (2 cm)	medium to hot	open	14-18 min
			covered	12-15 min
Porterhouse, T-bone or sirloin steak (medium)	1 inch (2.5 cm)	medium-hot	open	15-20 min
			covered	10-15 min
	1 1/2 inches (4 cm)		open	18-22 min
Chuck blade steak (medium)	1 inch (2.5 cm)	medium	open	15-20 min
			covered	12-18 min
	2 1/2 inches (6 cm)	medium	open	55-65 min
			covered	50-60 min

LAMB				
Rib chops (medium)	1 inch (2.5 cm)	medium	open	20-25 min
			covered	15-18 min
Shoulder chops (medium)	1 inch (2.5 cm)	medium	open	22-28 min
			covered	18-22 min

PORK				
Cut or portion — placed 4 inches (10 cm) above heat	Weight or thickness	Temperature of barbecue	Barbecue cover	Approximate cooking times
Loin chops (well done)	1 inch (2.5 cm)	medium	open	22-25 min
			covered	18-22 min
Blade steak (well done)	3/4 inch (2 cm)	medium	open	15-20 min
			covered	12-18 min
Spare ribs (well done)	5-6 lb (2-3 kg)	medium	covered	1 1/4 hr

CHICKEN				
Broiler-fryer halves (well done)	2 1/2 lb (1.25 kg)	medium-hot	open	45-50 min
			covered	40-45 min
Roasting chicken, unstuffed (well done)	3-4 lb (2 kg)	medium	covered	2 - 2 1/2 hr

TURKEY				
Unstuffed	6-8 lb (3-4 kg)	medium	covered	3 - 3 3/4 hr
	12-16 lb (6-8 kg)	medium	covered	3 1/2 - 4 hr

FISH & SEAFOOD				
Salmon or halibut steaks (well done)	3/4 inch (2 cm)	medium	open	17-22 min
			covered	15-20 min
Trout, white fish or fillets (well done)	8 oz (250 g)	medium-hot	open	10-17 min
			covered	10-15 min
Shrimp (large)	2 lb (1 kg)	hot	open	15-18 min
			covered	10-15 min

Rotisserie Cooking Chart

Type of Meat	Cut	Weight	Heat	Time
BEEF	Roast, rolled rib	3-4 lb (1.5-2 kg)	medium	2 1/2 - 3 hr
	Roast, tenderloin	2-2 1/2 lb (1 kg)	medium-hot	30-40 min
	Roast, rump	3-4 lb (1.5-2 kg)	low	1 1/2 - 2 hr
PORK	Roast, boneless loin	4-6 lb (2-3 kg)	medium	4 - 4 1/2 hr
	Ribs, back or side	3-4 lb (1.5-2 kg)	low	1 1/2 - 2 hr
CHICKEN	Whole, unstuffed	2 1/2-3 1/2 lb (1-1.5 kg)	medium-hot	1 1/2 - 1 3/4 hr
	Whole, unstuffed	6-8 lb (3-4 kg)	medium	2 1/2 - 3 hr
	Cornish hens (2)	1-2 lb (.5-1 kg)	medium-hot	1 1/2 - 3 hr
TURKEY	Whole, unstuffed	8-10 lb (4-5 kg)	medium	3-3 1/2 hr
DUCK	Whole, unstuffed	4-6 lb (2-2.5 kg)	medium-hot	1 1/2-2 hr
FISH	Whole	3-4 lb (1.5-2 kg)	medium-hot	25-45 min

Marinades, Glazes & Sauces

Candy may be dandy, liquor undoubtedly quicker, but it truly is the sauce that carries you off (apologies to Ogden Nash).

Marinades, glazes, and sauces all play an important role in barbecuing. They can be applied to food before, during, and after cooking. Marinades impart flavour and tenderness to most meats, poultry, and seafood. Cheaper, less tender cuts of meat such as chuck or flank steak benefit greatly from marinating. Always use glass, plastic, or stainless steel containers for marinades because the acid from citrus juices and vinegars can absorb metallic flavours from aluminum and other reactive metals. You can line a bowl or pan with a plastic bag to hold both food and marinades. Not only does this trick enable the marinade to cover all surfaces of the meat, but it makes for a quick and easy cleanup.

Marinades should not be reused. After food has been removed from a marinade, it can be used to baste the meat during cooking. Other than that, leftover marinade must be thrown away or boiled well before using on food hot off the grill.

Glazes are usually brushed on during the last 10 minutes of cooking. Often sweet and sticky, they provide a contrast to the smoky flavour of the barbecued meat. Because most glazes have a high sugar content, they may cause charring if left too long over intense heat. Flare-ups can also result from glazes dripping on hot coals.

Sauces may include popular standbys like mustard and ketchup. Mayonnaise, chutneys, salsas, conserves, relishes, herb butters, and oils are all served with food to enhance flavours. Use your imagination, and try different combinations. You may be used to eating horseradish with roast beef — why not try it with salmon? You'll be surprised at how many new favourites you discover.

Spice Rub for Lamb

MAKES 1/2 CUP (125 ML)

My grandmother used spice rubs for pork and ham, which she would simmer for hours in the oven. Rubs are popular again and are a great way to add flavour to barbecued meats such as beef, pork, lamb, and poultry. This one is especially delicious on lamb.

— R

1/4 cup	chopped fresh basil	50 ml
1/4 cup	chopped fresh parsley	50 ml
2 tsp	chopped fresh rosemary	10 ml
2	garlic cloves, chopped finely	2
1 tsp	black peppercorns, crushed	5 ml
1 tsp	mustard seeds, crushed	5 ml
	zest of 1 lemon	
	olive oil, to moisten	

Combine everything but the olive oil in a food processor or mortar and pestle, and grind coarsely. Add just enough oil to make a paste. Rub well onto the meat before grilling.

Citrus zest, the fragrant outermost layer of skin from citrus fruit, can be removed with a sharp paring knife, a vegetable peeler, a grater, or a special tool called a zester, and it may take the form of strips or shreds. Remove only the coloured layer of skin containing the fragrant oils, not the bitter white pith underneath. Zest can be added directly to most recipes.

Sesame Ginger Rub

MAKES 1/3 CUP (75 ML)

If sesame seeds are not already toasted, toss in a frying pan over medium heat, until lightly brown and fragrant. Remove from heat.

This rub can be used on chicken, white fish, or pork.

– R & W

1/4 cup	toasted sesame seeds	50 ml
1 Tbsp	grated fresh ginger	15 ml
2 Tbsp	chopped fresh basil	30 ml
2	garlic cloves, diced	2
1/2 tsp	sugar	2 ml
	pinch of cayenne pepper	

Combine sesame seeds, ginger, basil, garlic, sugar and cayenne in a bowl or mortar, and grind together using the back of a metal spoon or a pestle. Pat the mixture onto lightly oiled fish or meat before grilling.

Moshe's Marinating Oil

MAKES 1 1/2 CUPS (375 ML)

This exquisite but simple oil is the brainchild of our friend Moshe, who is originally from Tehran and revels in food cooked with herbs and spices. The oil should be kept in a sealed container and can be topped up as required. We use it to marinate chicken, pork, or beef prior to grilling. I even baste meat with this oil as it cooks on the grill.

– R

1 1/2 cups	olive oil	375 ml
4	garlic cloves, chopped finely	4
2	small hot chili peppers, chopped finely	2
6	black peppercorns, crushed	6
1/4 tsp	mustard seeds, crushed	1 ml
1/4 tsp	coriander seeds, crushed	1 ml
1 tsp	paprika	5 ml

In a glass or crockery container with a tightly fitting lid, combine all ingredients. Mix well and leave for a week or more before using.

Ginger Citrus Marinade

MAKES ABOUT 1/3 CUP (75 ML)

This delicious marinade is perfect for scallops, salmon fillets or steaks. Make sure to use a glass or ceramic dish, as the citrus juice will react with aluminum, causing an unpleasant taste and colour.

– R & W

1/4 cup	lime or lemon juice	50 ml
2 Tbsp	canola oil	30 ml
1	garlic clove, diced	1
1 Tbsp	grated fresh ginger	15 ml
1/4 tsp	salt	1 ml
	pinch cayenne pepper	

In a shallow glass bowl or dish, mix all ingredients well. Place fish into marinade and coat thoroughly by turning once or twice. Cover and refrigerate for at least one hour before removing and grilling fish according to recipe.

Piquant Orange Glaze

MAKES 1 1/4 CUPS (300 ML)

This zesty glaze works wonders with pork, lamb, or duck. Use it as a basting glaze during the last few minutes of cooking, or dress the cooked meat with it, just before serving.

— R & W

2 Tbsp	orange zest	30 ml
1 Tbsp	corn syrup	15 ml
1 Tbsp	apple cider vinegar	15 ml
1 cup	chicken or vegetable stock or broth	250 ml
1/4 cup	frozen orange juice concentrate	50 ml
1 Tbsp	cornstarch	15 ml
1/4 cup	Grand Marnier or other orange liqueur	50 ml
1 tsp	salt	5 ml

In a small saucepan, combine orange zest, corn syrup, vinegar, broth or stock, and orange juice concentrate. Bring to a boil and cook for about 5 minutes. Remove from heat, dissolve cornstarch with a small amount of orange liquid, and mix into the sauce, stirring well. Simmer until slightly thickened. Remove from heat and add Grand Marnier, stirring well. Add salt to taste. Serve hot, or use as a glaze during the last few minutes of cooking.

Maritime Barbecue Sauce

MAKES 2 CUPS (500 ML)

Nothing says "the Maritimes" like molasses and beer, so this is a true Down East union.

– R & W

1/2 cup	chopped onions	125 ml
3 Tbsp	canola oil	45 ml
2 Tbsp	Worcestershire Sauce	30 ml
2 tsp	salt	10 ml
2 tsp	dry mustard	10 ml
6 oz	tomato sauce	175 ml
1/2 tsp	freshly ground black pepper	2 ml
3/4 cup	beer	175 ml
3/4 tsp	chili powder	3 ml
3 Tbsp	apple cider vinegar	45 ml
1	garlic clove, diced	1
3 Tbsp	molasses	45 ml

In a small, heavy saucepan, sauté onions in canola oil. Add remaining ingredients and mix well. Cook over low heat until sauce thickens. Use to baste hamburgers, spare ribs or hot dogs, or pour over meatballs and bake in a low oven until sauce is thick and meat is cooked through.

Plum and Ginger Sauce

MAKES 1 CUP (250 ML)

This plum sauce, great with barbecued pork, beef, chicken, or lamb, is best used as a glaze during the last few minutes of cooking. It is especially good with Far East Pork (page 142).

– R & W

1 Tbsp	canola oil	15 ml
2	garlic cloves, chopped finely	2
1 Tbsp	grated fresh ginger	15 ml
2 Tbsp	brown sugar	30 ml
2 Tbsp	apple cider vinegar	30 ml
3/4 cup	plum jam or preserves	175 ml
1/4 cup	tomato sauce	50 ml
1/2 tsp	cayenne pepper	2 ml
	pinch of salt	

In a small saucepan over medium heat, sauté oil and garlic for 1 minute. Add ginger and brown sugar, stirring well. Add vinegar, plum jam or preserves, and tomato sauce, stirring well. Bring to a boil and remove from heat. Add cayenne pepper and salt, stir to mix, and let cool.

Flavoured Butters

Flavoured butters are easy to make. They are delicious sliced onto grilled meats, fish, and vegetables; melted and used for basting; or as a quick way to flavour sauces.
– R & W

1/2 cup	unsalted butter, softened	125 ml

In a small bowl, mix softened butter with any of the flavourings described below. Spoon onto a sheet of waxed paper or aluminum foil, and shape the butter into a log by rolling the paper into a cylinder. Close the ends with a twist, and refrigerate until firm. These butters can be frozen for several months if tightly wrapped. Use in any recipes that call for flavoured butters.

Herb Butter

2 Tbsp	minced fresh herbs	30 ml
1 tsp	lemon juice	5 ml
	salt and freshly ground black pepper	

Use on grilled vegetables, seafood, pork, beef, or poultry.

Garlic Butter

4 - 5	garlic cloves, minced	4 - 5
2 Tbsp	chopped parsley	30 ml
	freshly ground black pepper	

Melt as a dipping butter for lobster; place a slice on filet mignon; or, traditionally, spread on French bread.

Lemon Butter

	freshly squeezed juice and zest of 1/2 lemon	
	salt and freshly ground black pepper	

Use when basting lamb, pork, or fish.

Butter burns easily, so these flavoured butters should be used for basting foods that are quickly grilled.

Sesame Butter

2 Tbsp	lightly toasted sesame seeds	30 ml
1/8 tsp	sesame oil	.5 ml
1 Tbsp	chopped fresh cilantro	15 ml
	freshly ground black pepper	

Delicious on warm cornbread, or instead of garlic butter on French bread.

Nut Butter

1/3 cup	toasted nuts (such as hazelnuts, pecans, pine nuts), minced	75 ml
	salt and freshly ground black pepper	

Serve with lobster, crab, scallops, or shrimp.

Peach Chutney

When we make this at the Inn, guests and staff alike gravitate to the kitchen to find out what smells so good. It certainly spices up a pork chop, and is equally delicious on chicken, turkey, duck, and haddock.

– W

1/2 cup	apple cider vinegar	125 ml
1 cup	brown sugar	250 ml
5	peaches	5
1	lemon	1
1 cup	raisins	250 ml
1 Tbsp	grated fresh ginger	15 ml
2 tsp	minced garlic	10 ml
1/2 tsp	curry powder	2 ml
1/8 tsp	cayenne pepper	.5 ml
1/8 tsp	salt	.5 ml

Peel, pit and chop peaches. Chop the unpeeled lemon, discarding the seeds.

In a medium-sized saucepan, stir together vinegar and brown sugar over medium heat. Bring to a boil and add remaining ingredients, stirring well. Cook about 5 minutes, until sauce begins to thicken.

Remove from heat and use at once, or store in sterilized jars in the refrigerator for up to 2 weeks. Leftovers can be frozen as soon as chutney has cooled.

Red-Hot Tomato Sauce

MAKES 2 CUPS (500 ML)

2	red peppers	2
1	onion, top and bottom ends removed	1
2 1/2 lb	tomatoes	1.25 kg
1/3 cup	olive oil	75 ml
1 Tbsp	balsamic vinegar	15 ml
1/4 cup	chopped fresh basil	50 ml
1	garlic clove, crushed	1
1/2 tsp	hot sauce	2 ml
1/8 tsp	hot red pepper flakes	.5 ml
1/2 tsp	salt	2 ml
	freshly ground black pepper	

Take advantage of the abundance of tomatoes and peppers that appear in late summer to prepare this wonderful sauce. Serve it fresh over pasta or your favourite barbecued fish, or freeze it and remember the taste of summer in mid-January. Depending on the size of your grill, you can cook the vegetables all at once or grill them in batches.
– R & W

Preheat barbecue to hot, and oil the grill.

Brush the whole peppers, onion, and tomatoes with olive oil and place them on the grill. Turn them occasionally, cooking until charred all over. The peppers and onion will take 10-20 minutes, while the tomatoes will be ready in 2-4 minutes.

Place charred vegetables in a plastic bag until cool enough to peel. Remove charred skin, stems and seeds from peppers and tomatoes. Peel away the charred skins from onions. Chop vegetables into fine dice and combine in a large bowl. Add remaining olive oil, vinegar, basil, garlic, hot sauce, pepper flakes, salt, and pepper. Serve with grilled fish or pasta.

Tomato and Avocado Salsa

MAKES 2 1/2 CUPS (625 ML)

Avocado and tomato were destined for culinary matrimony. This wonderful salsa is delicious with grilled fish, lamb, or poultry. Let the salsa stand for 30 minutes before using, but don't leave longer than an hour or two, as oxidization will ruin the flavours by making them too intense.

– R & W

1 cup	diced ripe tomato	250 ml
1/2 cup	seeded and diced cucumber	125 ml
1/4 cup	diced red onion	50 ml
1	jalapeño pepper, seeded and chopped finely	1
1 Tbsp	lime juice	15 ml
1 Tbsp	rice vinegar	15 ml
1 Tbsp	chopped fresh parsley	15 ml
1 tsp	salt	5 ml
1	large avocado, pitted, peeled, and diced	1

In a glass bowl, mix all ingredients except avocado. Add avocado and toss lightly to blend. Let stand about 20-30 minutes before using.

Green Tomato Salsa

MAKES 4 CUPS (1 L)

This salsa is great with either green or ripe red tomatoes. Yellow tomatoes are also fine. This condiment is especially good served with grilled shark or tuna.

– R & W

Whichever tomato you decide to try, use the opposite colour pepper to add contrast. More jalapeño pepper can be added if you like an extra hot zing.

3 cups	seeded and chopped tomatoes	750 ml
1/2 cup	chopped green or red pepper	125 ml
1/2 cup	chopped onion	125 ml
3 Tbsp	chopped fresh cilantro	45 ml
1	jalapeño pepper, seeded and chopped	1
3	garlic cloves, chopped	3
1/2 tsp	salt	2 ml
3 Tbsp	lime juice	45 ml

Mix all ingredients in a glass bowl and let marinate in the refrigerator for about 1 hour before serving.

Cilantro Yogurt Sauce

MAKES 1 1/2 CUPS (375 ML)

This is a creamy, mild sauce if the pepper is omitted, but a little chopped jalapeño adds a nice contrast to the cool yogurt. Either way, it's delicious served with pork, chicken, or fish, or as a dip for vegetables.

– R & W

1/2 cup	finely chopped fresh cilantro	125 ml
1	garlic clove, minced	1
1/4	jalapeño pepper, seeded and chopped finely	1/4
1 tsp	salt	5 ml
1 cup	plain yogurt	250 ml

Combine all ingredients in a medium-sized bowl. Chill.

Minted Yogurt Sauce

MAKES 2 CUPS (500 ML)

Mint grows like a weed in most gardens, so you might as well enjoy it in as many recipes as possible. Whenever we serve lamb, we think mint. This savoury recipe is a nice change from the usual sweet jelly.

– W

2	garlic cloves, mashed	2
1/2 tsp	salt	2 ml
1/4 cup	fresh mint leaves, chopped	50 ml
2 cups	plain yogurt	500 ml
1/4 tsp	sugar	1 ml
1/4 tsp	lemon zest	1 ml

In the small bowl of a food processor, purée garlic and salt. Add mint, pulsing until minced finely. Combine yogurt with sugar, lemon zest and mint mixture. Mix well. Refrigerate until ready to serve.

Mustard Dill Sauce

MAKES 1 CUP (250 ML)

Cold smoked salmon, thinly sliced and served with small pieces of rye bread — a marriage meant to last when anointed with this delectable sauce. It requires a fair amount of whisking to properly emulsify the oil and vinegar, but the results are worth the exercise. Fresh dill is essential.

– R & W

3 Tbsp	grainy Dijon mustard	45 ml
2 Tbsp	red wine vinegar	30 ml
1 Tbsp	liquid honey	15 ml
3/4 cup	canola or olive oil	175 ml
1/3 cup	fresh dill, chopped	75 ml
	salt and freshly ground black pepper	

In a stainless steel bowl, beat the mustard, vinegar, and honey, using a wire whisk. Place bowl on a wet dishcloth to keep it steady while you are whisking. Continue whisking while gradually pouring the oil in a steady stream into the other ingredients. The mixture should resemble a light mayonnaise when fully emulsified. Add chopped dill and salt and pepper to taste.

Mayonnaise

MAKES ABOUT 1 1/2 CUPS (375 ML)

Mum always made her own mayonnaise, although we called it salad dressing. It was wonderful on cold poached salmon and on the green lettuce she grew herself. Try making it at least once each summer. The homemade flavour is worth the extra effort.

– W

2	egg yolks	2
	pinch each of salt and white pepper	
1 tsp	Dijon mustard	5 ml
2 Tbsp	white wine vinegar or freshly squeezed lemon juice	30 ml
1 1/2 cups	vegetable oil	375 ml
1 Tbsp	warm water (if needed)	15 ml

In a medium-sized bowl, whisk or beat egg yolks with salt and pepper, mustard, and 1 Tbsp (15 ml) vinegar or lemon juice. Whisk or beat in 2-3 Tbsp (30-45 ml) of the oil, a drop at a time. Add the remaining oil in a very fine stream, whisking constantly. Stir in the remaining vinegar.

Taste and adjust for seasoning. If the mayonnaise is too thick, gradually beat in the warm water. Store in a clean, covered jar in the refrigerator for up to one week.

Food Processor or Blender Mayonnaise

Process a whole egg (rather than 2 yolks) with salt and pepper, mustard, 1 Tbsp (15 ml) vinegar, and 1 Tbsp (15 ml) oil until well blended. Keep machine running while gradually adding the rest of the oil. Add the remaining vinegar and process until smooth.

Herb Mayonnaise

Add 1 Tbsp (15 ml) freshly chopped herb of your choice to 1/2 cup (125 ml) mayonnaise.

Aïoli

To make this classic Provençal sauce, simply add 5-6 cloves of crushed garlic to the mayonnaise, and then cover and refrigerate. Aïoli is wonderful with grilled vegetables or fish.

Peanut Sauce

MAKES 1/2 CUP (125 ML)

This Asian-style sauce is wonderful with pork or chicken. My original recipe called for a number of exotic ingredients for which I have substituted more readily available seasonings. The next time you make a Caesar salad, try adding grilled strips of chicken or pork dressed with this spicy peanut sauce.

– R

3 Tbsp	peanut butter	45 ml
1 Tbsp	red wine or cider vinegar	15 ml
1 Tbsp	soy sauce	15 ml
1 Tbsp	liquid honey	15 ml
1	garlic clove, finely chopped	1
1/4 tsp	sesame oil	1 ml
1 tsp	powdered ginger	5 ml
	or	
1 Tbsp	grated fresh ginger	15 ml
1 tsp	hot pepper sauce	5 ml
3 Tbsp	white wine, water, or apple juice	45 ml
1/2 tsp	salt	2 ml

In a small saucepan, mix all ingredients and cook over medium heat until bubbling hot. Add a little more wine, water, or apple juice to thin the sauce if you wish. Serve over sliced cooked pork or chicken.

Herbed Cheese

Cream cheese is a versatile food to keep in the refrigerator. This flavoured cheese can be served on toast or bagels or on grilled vegetables or meat.

– W

8 oz	cream cheese, softened	250 g
2 Tbsp	chopped fresh parsley	30 ml
1 Tbsp	chopped fresh chives	15 ml
2 tsp	chopped fresh oregano	10 ml
1/2	garlic clove, minced	1/2
	pinch of cayenne pepper	

In a small bowl, mix cream cheese with other ingredients until well blended. Cover and refrigerate until ready to use.

Seafood Dressing

MAKES 1 1/2 CUPS (375 ML)

This recipe was invented during the taping of Tide's Table, *our television cooking show. We had finished all our scheduled recipes when we were told we still had five minutes to fill. Ross sat down at the computer and created this dressing for seafood.*

– W

1/4 cup	mayonnaise	50 ml
2 Tbsp	chopped green onion	30 ml
2 Tbsp	chopped fresh parsley	30 ml
1 cup	chili sauce	250 ml
2 Tbsp	diced celery	30 ml
1 tsp	Worcestershire Sauce	5 ml
2	gherkin pickles, diced	2

In a glass bowl, mix all ingredients and serve as a dipping sauce for clams, mussels and lobster.

Tartar Sauce

We really like tartar sauce with fish and chips or fried clams, but this sauce is equally delicious with any barbecued or grilled fish or chicken. It's also good as a vegetable dip. Change the mustard variety and you change the flavour of the sauce: tarragon mustard is excellent with chicken, and whole grain Dijon goes well with salmon.

– R & W

1 cup	mayonnaise	250 ml
1 Tbsp	herb mustard	15 ml
2 Tbsp	chopped fresh parsley	30 ml
1 Tbsp	finely chopped mild onion	15 ml
1 Tbsp	capers, drained, rinsed, and chopped	15 ml
1 Tbsp	finely chopped gherkin pickles	15 ml
1 tsp	Worcestershire Sauce	5 ml
1 tsp	lemon juice	5 ml
	salt and pepper	

In a medium-sized bowl, mix mayonnaise and mustard until well blended. Add parsley, onion, capers, pickles, Worcestershire Sauce and lemon juice. Add salt and pepper to taste.

Cover and refrigerate for 2-4 days.

Béarnaise Sauce

MAKES 3/4 CUP (175 ML)

This classic sauce is the perfect accompaniment for beef tenderloin or filet (see page 96). The subtle use of tarragon will enhance rather than mask the delicate flavour of the beef.

– R & W

It is important to keep the pan temperature low while thickening the sauce. If the sauce begins to separate, remove from heat, whisk in 1 Tbsp (15 ml) cold water, and then return to heat.

1/4 cup	white wine vinegar	50 ml
1/4 cup	dry white wine	50 ml
2 Tbsp	chopped green onions	30 ml
1 Tbsp	chopped fresh tarragon leaves	15 ml
3	egg yolks	3
1/8 tsp	salt	.5 ml
1/8 tsp	pepper (white, if available)	.5 ml
3/4 cup	melted butter	175 ml
1 Tbsp	finely chopped fresh parsley	15 ml
	tarragon for garnish	

In a large heavy saucepan, combine vinegar, wine, green onions, and chopped tarragon. Cook over medium heat 15-20 minutes until reduced by half. Set aside until cool. In a small bowl, whisk together egg yolks, salt, and pepper. Add to the cooled onion mixture, whisking until foamy. Place pan over low heat, and whisk constantly until mixture thickens slightly. Remove from heat and whisk in melted butter very slowly. Stir in parsley. Serve with tenderloin, garnished with tarragon sprigs.

Basil and Sour Cream Dip

MAKES 1 CUP (250 ML)

This versatile pesto-flavoured dip is wonderful to have on hand to keep guests happy while they are waiting for dinner. Have a platter of fresh veggies ready — cherry tomatoes, crisp pea pods, mushrooms, baby carrots, and zucchini sticks are all good choices. Add a cool drink and no one will notice if dinner is late.

— R & W

1 cup	sour cream	250 ml
1/2 cup	grated parmesan cheese	125 ml
1	garlic clove, chopped finely	1
1/4 tsp	salt	1 ml
1/2 tsp	lemon juice	2 ml
1/3 cup	chopped fresh basil leaves	75 ml

Using a food processor or blender, combine half the sour cream, parmesan cheese, and garlic. Blend until smooth. Add salt, lemon juice, and basil. Continue blending until mixture is creamy, 1-2 minutes. Add remaining sour cream, and blend quickly to mix. Pour into medium-sized bowl, cover, and refrigerate to chill, about 1 hour.

Fish & Shellfish

We have always referred to fish as "fast food," and certainly this holds true if you are cooking it on a gas or electric barbecue. Things slow down slightly if charcoal is involved, but that is simply because it takes longer to heat the grill; the fish cooks just as fast.

When we began barbecuing, fish was pretty much the underdog. Steak, pork chops, and a bit of chicken ruled the roost, so to speak. But with the growing popularity of seafood in general, and the ease with which it can be purchased —even inland — more and more barbecue recipes are devoted to seafood.

We have ignored a few varieties simply because some fish is too delicate for open grilling. Flounder and sole can be prepared in foil, which in the end is akin to oven cooking. Shellfish works best on skewers. Shrimp and scallops make delicious kabobs, alone or with vegetables or fruit. Firm-fleshed fish such as salmon, halibut and swordfish, cook as easily as meat directly on the grill, but they also do well on skewers. In addition to serving boiled or steamed lobster, we use lobster as a special stuffing rather than cooking it directly on the barbecue, where its delicate flavour is often lost and its meat dries out.

Fear of overcooking has discouraged many people from trying fish either on the grill or in their kitchens, and dry fish does become rather tasteless. However, if you follow the simple guideline of no more than 10 minutes per inch (2.5 cm) of thickness, you should be left with tender, juicy seafood. However, the best rule of thumb is that fish is done when it is opaque or can be easily flaked with a fork. Squeeze on some fresh lemon juice and dinner's ready.

Fish and seafood can be cooked to advantage in the barbecue by open grilling, rotisserie cooking, or foil baking. Firm-fleshed varieties of fish — salmon, halibut, haddock, cod, tuna, Arctic char, sturgeon, shark and catfish — are suited to grilling. Softer-fleshed fish, such as sole, flounder, pike, pickerel, and perch, are best cooked in foil or a rotisserie basket. Clams, mussels, and oysters are most succulent when cooked right in their shells on the grill or when steamed in a covered pan containing water, broth, and white wine with herbs.

Bacon Wrapped Trout

SERVES 4-6

Use the flat edge of a knife to flatten and stretch bacon slices to ensure easy wrapping.

Rainbow, brook, or cut throat trout are all superb when grilled on the barbecue, and they will stay moist and juicy if wrapped in bacon. Be sure the fish is as fresh as possible.

– R & W

6	whole trout, heads and tails attached	6
	salt and freshly ground black pepper	
6	lemon slices	6
6-12	slices bacon	6-12

Preheat barbecue to medium-hot.

Wash cleaned trout and pat dry. Sprinkle them inside with salt and pepper, and place a slice of lemon into each cavity. Wrap 1-2 slices of bacon around each fish, securing with toothpicks. When barbecue is hot, place fish on the grill. Close lid and grill about 4 minutes, until bacon is browned and sizzling. Turn and grill the other side for 4 minutes more. Serve hot.

Clay Baked Trout

SERVES 4

Growing up near the banks of the St. John River in New Brunswick and the Fraser River in British Columbia, we played with (and in) fresh water clay all summer long. We plastered wet clay to our bodies, emulating posh spa treatments. When that grew tiresome, we fashioned clay pots and baked them in the sun or campfires, hoping to sell them for a fortune. And when we caught a fish, we would often wrap it in leaves, surround the package with clay, and bake it in an open fire. In principle, clay baking is not unlike cooking in covered ceramic or pottery dishes. The difference is that in clay baking the heat first bakes and hardens the clay in which the food is encased. We simply waited until the lump of clay was hard enough to kick around the fire, and then gave it another 5 or 10 minutes or so. Then we removed the black lump of clay from the hot coals and broke it open. The contents would be pronounced perfect, regardless.

– R & W

2-3 lb	whole sea trout, cleaned	1-1.5 kg
	salt and freshly ground pepper	

Preheat barbecue to hot.

Wash fish and pat dry. Sprinkle cavity with salt and pepper. On a sheet of aluminum foil, pat or roll out half the clay, until about 3/4 inch (1.5 cm) thick and slightly larger than the fish itself. Place fish in centre of clay. Roll out remaining clay and use to completely encase the fish. Pinch and smooth the seams to seal tightly. Using a pencil-sized stick, poke a hole in the top of the clay packet. This will allow steam to vent nicely so the clay will not bubble or crack during cooking. The hole can also

You can buy fresh clay from any local potter or potters' supply store. It is perfectly safe and contains no harmful chemicals. You'll need about 2 pounds (1 kg) for a fish of the same weight.

accommodate an instant-read thermometer when you wish to check the internal temperature of the fish.

Transfer foil, clay, and fish onto the barbecue grill, and reduce heat to medium. Close the lid, and bake 15-20 minutes. When the clay has firmed up, it can be removed from the foil and placed directly on the grill. Cook with the lid closed for 10 minutes more, and then insert the thermometer to check the temperature. Fish is cooked when the temperature reaches 170°F (77°C).

Carefully remove to a wooden carving board. Crack the clay gently, using the handle of a kitchen knife or a small hammer, and pull away the top covering from the fish. The skin will come away with the clay, leaving a delicious, moist sea trout ready to serve.

Spinach Stuffed Rainbow Trout

SERVES 2

The taste of this trout takes me back to my childhood, when I frequently caught rainbow trout in a creek close to my home. Although times have changed and wild trout are not as readily available, farmed rainbow trout are equally tasty with this flavourful and healthy stuffing.

– R

A grilling basket is a handy utensil for cooking stuffed fish, as it prevents the stuffing from falling out and makes for easy turning. If you don't have one, simply wrap the stuffed fish in aluminum foil before grilling.

1 Tbsp	butter	15 ml
1	spring onion, chopped	1
1 cup	chopped spinach	250 ml
1/2 cup	bread crumbs	125 ml
2 Tbsp	grated parmesan cheese	30 ml
	dash of milk or cream	
	salt and pepper	
4	small trout, cleaned	4
1 Tbsp	canola oil	15 ml

Preheat barbecue to medium-hot.

In a small frying pan, melt butter over medium-high heat. Add onion and chopped spinach, stirring to coat well. Cook only a moment or two to wilt the vegetables. Remove from heat and add bread crumbs, cheese, and milk or cream. Stir to incorporate. Season with salt and pepper to taste, and let cool slightly. Rub skins of trout lightly with canola oil. Stuff the cavities of the trout with the spinach mixture and place in grilling basket. Cook for 8-10 minutes, turning occasionally.

Trout in Corn Husks

When I was a kid we used to grill fish in corn husks over an open campfire. We would take a few cobs of fresh corn with us when we went fishing, just in case we got lucky. This cooking method also works extremely well on the barbecue. The corn husks burn and blacken on the outside but retain moisture inside, and the fish cooks in a most succulent fashion.

– R

While the trout is cooking, you can grill the ears of corn that came out of the husks. Roll them back and forth on the grill every few minutes. Butter, salt and pepper the corn during the last few minutes of cooking. Corn needs only to be hot and steaming to be ready for eating.

4	small trout (cleaned) or boneless fillets	4
1 Tbsp	butter or canola oil	15 ml
1 Tbsp	chopped fresh parsley	15 ml
4	fresh corn husks, silks removed	4
	salt and freshly ground black pepper	

Preheat barbecue to hot.

Sprinkle fish with melted butter or oil. Salt and pepper lightly and sprinkle with chopped parsley. Place prepared fish inside empty corn husks. Twist husks together at each end and secure with fine wire or non-plastic twist ties. Place on hot barbecue and close lid. Cook for 15 minutes, turning husks halfway through cooking. Carefully remove blackened husks from grill. Let cool slightly before opening husk ends. Peel back hot husks and serve.

Planked Salmon

This cooking method produces succulent results. It can also be done in the oven, or it can be propped in front of a large, hot, open fire if you've run out of propane. Soak a length of raw, unpainted maple or cedar plank in cold water for about 30 minutes before cooking. The wood should be 1-2 inches (2.5-5 cm) thick, and large enough to hold your salmon fillet.

– R

2 lb	boneless, skinned salmon fillet	1 kg
1/4 cup	canola or olive oil	50 ml
1 Tbsp	brown sugar	15 ml
	grated zest and juice of 1 lemon	
1 Tbsp	fresh chopped dill or chives	15 ml
2 tsp	freshly ground black pepper	10 ml

Soak plank in cold water. In a small bowl, combine oil, sugar, lemon juice and zest, fresh herbs, and pepper. Rub salmon fillet with mixture. Let fish marinate for about 30 minutes.

Preheat barbecue to hot.

Place two bricks on the grill, positioned to hold the plank. Ten minutes before cooking salmon, put wet plank on bricks, and close the lid. Carefully place marinated salmon on hot plank. Close barbecue, cooking for 8-10 minutes per inch (2.5 cm) thickness of fish. Salmon is done when it flakes easily when prodded with a fork.

Dilled Salmon Steaks

SERVES 4

Now that Atlantic salmon is being farmed, it is readily available across the country. We recently celebrated Valentine's Day with dinner at a gourmet restaurant in Palm Desert, California. Imagine our surprise when we were told Bay of Fundy salmon was one of the house specialtiess!

— R & W

1/2 cup	melted butter or margarine	125 ml
2 tsp	lemon juice	10 ml
2 tsp	fresh chopped dillweed	10 ml
	freshly ground black pepper	
4	salmon steaks, 1 inch (2.5 cm) thick	4
1	lemon, cut in wedges	1

Preheat barbecue to medium-hot.

In a small bowl, mix together butter or margarine, lemon juice, dill, and pepper. Brush salmon generously with butter, and place on oiled grill. Cook for 5 minutes. Turn steaks, and brush again with butter. Cook 5-6 more minutes, or until salmon flakes easily when prodded with a fork.

To serve, drizzle each steak with extra dill butter, and place a lemon wedge on the side.

Spicy Maple Salmon

SERVES 4

Maple syrup and salmon make an unusual but wonderful combination when united on the barbecue or in the smokehouse. Spicy but sweet, grilled maple-glazed salmon has a smoky flavour reminiscent of the many fish I've smoked over the years. Homemade smokehouses — looking like large phone booths or small outhouses — have adorned our backyard on more than one occasion. Until I got smart and built a sturdy unit out of corrugated iron, these smoke shacks had a tendency to catch fire and burn to the ground. After some three dozen smokings had made the shingled structure tinder-dry, it was not uncommon to see me running wildly into the backyard to retrieve a load of fish from the blazing inferno. This barbecue recipe provides the wonderful flavour of maple-smoked salmon with no smokehouse fires to worry about.

– R

1 cup	maple syrup	250 ml
1	small onion, chopped	1
2 Tbsp	apple cider vinegar	30 ml
2 Tbsp	Worcestershire Sauce	30 ml
1-2 tsp	hot pepper sauce	5-10 ml
1 tsp	dry mustard	5 ml
1 tsp	salt	5 ml
4	1/3-lb (175-g) boneless salmon fillets, with skin	4

Preheat barbecue to medium-hot.

Prepare sauce by combining everything except salmon in a small pan over medium heat. Stir until mixture boils. Reduce heat and simmer for about 4-5 minutes. Sauce can be cooled and refrigerated in a sealed container for about 10 days.

Oil grill, and place salmon fillets skin-side up. Close barbecue lid, and cook for 3-4 minutes. Carefully turn fillets, and, using a pastry or barbecue brush, paint maple syrup mixture on salmon. Close lid, and cook 3-4 minutes more, watching for flare-ups. Fish is ready when it flakes easily when prodded with a fork. Turn off barbecue, lift fillets from grill and serve on a warmed platter.

Fillets with skins attached keep their shape better than skinless fillets. The cooked fish will easily separate from the skin for serving.

Oriental Salmon

SERVES 4

The Japanese excel in preparing seafood. These salmon steaks must marinate for about an hour before grilling. Be sure to use Japanese soy sauce rather than the traditional Chinese product, which is heavily salted. The sweeter, more delicate flavour of Japanese soy sauce is exquisite in this recipe.

–R & W

1/2 cup	Japanese-style soy sauce	125 ml
1/4 cup	brown sugar	50 ml
3/4 cup	Dubonnet or dry sherry	175 ml
3	green onions, chopped	3
4	Atlantic salmon steaks, 1 1/2 inches (4 cm) thick	4

In a glass baking dish, mix soy sauce, sugar, wine, and green onions. Place salmon steaks into mixture, and marinate for one hour, turning occasionally.

Preheat barbecue to medium-hot.

Place the steaks in a lightly oiled fish basket, and grill about 12 minutes, basting with reserved marinade and turning occasionally. Serve on a bed of hot rice.

Barbecue-Smoked Salmon

SERVES 4

Brining overnight is important before smoking fish in a barbecue. The brining process firms the flesh and imparts a sweet saltiness that blends well with the flavour of wood smoke. Almost any type of fruit or hardwood chips works well in a barbecue smoker. If your grill does not have a smoke pan, simply use a metal pie plate or shallow baking pan to hold the wood.

– R & W

2 lb	salmon fillets, 1 inch (2.5 cm) thick, with skin	1 kg
4 cups	water	1 L
1/2 cup	brown sugar	125 ml
1/2 cup	coarse pickling salt	125 ml
1 Tbsp	freshly ground black pepper	15 ml

The night before you plan to smoke the fish, mix water, sugar, salt and pepper in a bowl, and stir until the sugar is dissolved. Lay salmon fillets in a glass baking dish, and pour brine solution over them. Cover with plastic wrap and refrigerate overnight. Turn fish once before retiring for the night, and again first thing the next morning. Before noon, remove fish from brine, and rinse quickly in cold water. Pat fillets dry, and lay them on paper towel to air-dry for about 1 hour. The fish will have a slightly tacky glaze. It is now ready to smoke.

Preheat barbecue to low. Put smoke pan with wood chips directly on lava rocks or ceramic cooking tiles, and close the lid. Once wood chips start to smoke, place the fish, skin-side down, on a rack, and set 6-8 inches (15-20 cm) above grill surface, using bricks to support the rack. Close lid and smoke for about 1-2 hours. Fish is ready when it flakes easily when prodded with a fork. Serve as an appetizer, either hot or cold. Fish smoked in this manner will keep for up to 1 week in the refrigerator.

Salmon Steaks in Citrus Yogurt
SERVES 4

This easy, low-fat marinade enhances the sweet, juicy flavour of Atlantic salmon steaks. Ginger, garlic, and citrus blend together to work their magic, creating another memorable meal from the ocean.

– R & W

4	salmon steaks	4
1/2 cup	plain low-fat yogurt	125 ml
1 Tbsp	vegetable oil	15 ml
	juice and zest of 1 lemon	
2 tsp	brown sugar	10 ml
1 Tbsp	grated fresh ginger	15 ml
1	garlic clove, minced	1
1/4 tsp	salt	1 ml
	lemon wedges for garnish	

Place salmon steaks in shallow glass container.

In a small bowl, mix together yogurt and everything else but the lemon wedges. Pour over salmon, turning fish to coat both sides. Cover and leave 3-4 hours.

Preheat barbecue to medium-hot.

Place salmon on oiled grill. Cook 5 minutes, and then turn and brush with marinade. Cook 5 minutes more, or until done to your taste. Serve with lemon wedges.

Salmon and Haddock Duo

SERVES 4

*Two of the finest fish are joined together in this simple recipe.
Don't you often find the simple things are the most memorable?*

– R & W

1/4 cup	melted butter	50 ml
1 tsp	vegetable oil	5 ml
1 Tbsp	lemon juice	15 ml
1	garlic clove, minced	1
1/4 tsp	grated fresh ginger	1 ml
1/2 lb	salmon fillet, cut into 1 1/2-inch (3.5-cm) cubes	250 g
1/2 lb	haddock fillet, cut into 1 1/2-inch (3.5-cm) cubes	250 g

In a small bowl, mix butter, oil, lemon juice, garlic, and ginger.
Preheat grill to medium-hot, and place two bricks on grill.

On oiled skewers, alternate salmon and haddock cubes, leaving
space so fish will cook evenly. Brush fish with butter mixture. Place
skewers on bricks above grill surface. Cook for 10 minutes, turning occasionally. Fish is done when it flakes when prodded with a fork.

Foiled Haddock

SERVES 4

We prefer haddock or cod, but you can use any fish you like with this recipe.

– R & W

1 1/2 lb	haddock fillets	750 g
1/4 lb	spinach leaves	125 g
1/4 cup	grated Swiss cheese	50 ml
1 Tbsp	butter	15 ml
2 Tbsp	chopped onion	30 ml
1/2 cup	sliced mushrooms	125 ml
1/2	lemon, sliced	1/2
	salt and freshly ground black pepper	

Preheat grill to hot.

Lay half the fillets on a double thickness of aluminium foil, sprayed with non-stick cooking spray. Lightly salt and pepper the fish, and place spinach leaves on top. Spread with half the grated cheese. Layer the rest of the fish on top of the spinach. Cover with onion, mushrooms and remainder of grated cheese. Top with lemon slices. Bring foil sides together and double-fold tightly. Fold ends to form a tightly sealed packet. Carefully place on grill, and close cover. Cook 20 minutes. The contents should be sizzling when removed from the grill. Open packet carefully to let steam escape. Serve immediately.

Skewered Haddock with Zesty Mayonnaise

SERVES 4

The delicate sweetness of haddock is brought out when this fish is grilled on the barbecue. Serve with a zesty herb mayonnaise.
– R & W

1 1/2 lb	haddock fillets, cut in 2-inch (5-cm) cubes	750 g
1/4 cup	canola oil	50 ml
1/2 cup	mayonnaise	125 ml
1 tsp	lemon zest	5 ml
3 Tbsp	lemon juice	45 ml
1 Tbsp	chopped fresh basil (or 1 tsp dried)	15 ml
	salt and pepper to taste	
	lemon wedges (optional)	

Soak bamboo skewers in water 1 hour before barbecuing.
Place two bricks on grill, and preheat barbecue to medium-hot.
Thread haddock cubes onto skewers. Brush lightly with canola oil. Meanwhile, mix mayonnaise, lemon zest and juice, and basil in a small bowl. Brush skewered fish with mayonnaise mixture and lay skewers on bricks above grill. Cook for 4-5 minutes, and turn carefully, using a metal spatula to avoid breaking fish. Baste and cook 4 more minutes. Serve hot with lemon wedges, if desired.

Zippy Haddock Fillets

SERVES 4

1/4 cup	mayonnaise	50 ml
	juice and zest of 1 lemon	
	dash of Tabasco Sauce	
1/2 tsp	fresh oregano, chopped	2 ml
2 Tbsp	fresh parsley, chopped	30 ml
4	fresh haddock fillets	4
2 Tbsp	vegetable oil	30 ml
1/2 tsp	salt	2 ml
1/4 tsp	freshly ground black pepper	1 ml

Preheat barbecue to medium-hot.

In a small bowl, mix mayonnaise, lemon juice and 1/2 tsp (2 ml) zest, Tabasco Sauce, oregano, and parsley. Set aside.

Brush fillets with oil and sprinkle with salt and pepper. Place on oiled grill, and close lid. Cook 3-4 minutes, turn and brush with oil, and cook 2 minutes more. Spread fillets with mayonnaise sauce. Turn and cook 1 minute. Baste again with sauce, and then turn and cook 1 minute more, or until fish flakes when prodded with a fork.

My dad once had a fish stall in the Saint John City Market, and he and my grandfather exported fish to the eastern United States. When fresh haddock is not available we often substitute halibut. Haddock certainly found its way to our table more than any other fish. It's my personal favourite.

– W

Maritime Burgers

When serving fish in a sandwich, it is very important to make sure there are no bones. Use a sharp knife or needle nose pliers to remove any stray bones before cooking.

Here in the Maritimes we are blessed year round with a supply of fresh fish of many varieties. For a delicious break from the usual beef burgers, we make these Maritime Burgers using whatever fish we have a hankering for, cod, haddock, or halibut. We try and keep the fish simple to avoid masking its wonderful flavour.

– R & W

2 Tbsp	lemon juice	30 ml
1 Tbsp	canola oil	15 ml
1 1/2 lb	haddock fillets, halved	750 g
6	kaiser rolls, halved	6
	butter	
6	tomato slices	6
	lettuce, arugula or watercress	
	mayonnaise or tartar sauce	

Preheat grill to medium-hot.

In a small dish, mix lemon juice and oil. Brush onto fish pieces and place on oiled grill. Cook for 5-6 minutes, brush with remaining oil and lemon juice, and carefully turn, cooking 4-5 minutes longer.

Meanwhile, toast and lightly butter sliced rolls. Remove fish from grill, cut fillets into serving-sized portions, and place on rolls. Add choice of greens and Mayonnaise (page 40) or Tartar Sauce (page 45).

Foil Grilled Cod and Veggies

SERVES 4

Ross always preferred eating cod when he lived on the West Coast, and although he loves haddock, he still gets a yearning for cod. When we find it fresh, this is one of our favourite ways to prepare it.

– W

Always be careful when opening foil packets cooked on the barbecue, as the steam may be very hot. Be sure to pour the tasty cooking juices over the fish.

1 lb	fresh cod fillets	500 g
2	medium zucchini, julienned	2
1	carrot, shredded	1
1	small onion, sliced thinly into rings	1
1/2 tsp	chopped fresh dill	2 ml
1/4 tsp	finely chopped garlic	1 ml
1/2 cup	grated white cheddar cheese	125 ml
	salt and freshly ground pepper	
1	lemon, cut in wedges	1

Preheat barbecue to medium-hot.

In the centre of an 18-inch (45-cm) square of heavy-duty aluminum foil, place cod fillets. Top with zucchini, carrot and onion. Sprinkle with dill, garlic, cheese, salt and pepper. Create a packet by folding in opposite sides of foil, crimping closed, and folding and tucking the open ends to seal. Place packet on barbecue and cook 10-15 minutes, until fish flakes when prodded with a fork.

Remove fish from foil, and place on platter. Garnish with lemon wedges.

Grilled Lemon Halibut

It has always been our practice to use fresh lemon whenever we cook seafood and to have a good-sized wedge on each plate. Lemon enhances rather than masks the flavour of fish and allows you to cut back on salt. Whenever you buy fish, stop at the produce counter and pick up a fresh lemon.

– R & W

2	garlic cloves, minced	2
	juice of 1 lemon	
	salt and freshly ground black pepper	
1/2 cup	olive oil	125 ml
1 Tbsp	soy sauce	15 ml
4	halibut steaks	4
1/4 cup	fresh chopped parsley	50 ml
1	lemon, cut in 4 wedges	1

Preheat barbecue to medium-hot.

In a small bowl, blend garlic, lemon juice, salt, pepper, oil, and soy sauce. Mix well.

Brush both sides of halibut steaks with sauce. Place on oiled grill and cook for 4-5 minutes. Carefully turn steaks over. Baste with sauce and cook 4-5 minutes more, basting frequently. Test for doneness by prodding centre bone. If it pulls away from the flesh easily, the fish is ready.

Place steaks on a warmed platter or on individual plates, and sprinkle with chopped parsley and remaining basting sauce. Garnish with lemon wedges to serve.

Halibut Steaks with Spicy Tomato Sauce

SERVES 4

2 Tbsp	butter	30 ml
1 cup	chopped onion	250 ml
1	garlic clove, minced	1
	salt and freshly ground black pepper	
4	large tomatoes, peeled and chopped	4
1/2 tsp	sugar	2 ml
1/4 tsp	hot sauce (Tabasco or your favourite)	1 ml
4	halibut steaks	4
1/4 cup	lemon juice	50 ml
2 Tbsp	melted butter	30 ml
2 Tbsp	dry sherry or red wine	30 ml
2 Tbsp	fresh chopped parsley	30 ml
2 Tbsp	freshly grated parmesan cheese	30 ml

Most barbecuing takes place in the summer, when we have an abundance of fresh tomatoes. This is a great fish dish to serve over pasta with freshly grated parmesan. Eggplant Stuffed Sweet Peppers (page 214) make a delicious accompaniment. A glass of wine and a basket of garlic bread complete this splendid warm-weather meal.
– R & W

In a small frying pan on the side burner of your barbecue, melt 2 Tbsp (30 ml) butter, add onion, and sauté over medium heat for 3 minutes, stirring constantly. Add garlic, and sauté until onion is lightly browned.

Add salt, pepper, tomatoes, sugar, and hot sauce. Cover and simmer for 15 minutes, stirring occasionally. Keep warm over low heat while preparing fish, or make in advance and reheat before using.

Preheat barbecue to medium-hot.

Rub halibut steaks with 2 Tbsp (30 ml) lemon juice, and let stand 10 minutes. Combine remaining 2 Tbsp (30 ml) lemon juice with 2 Tbsp (30 ml) melted butter.

Place steaks on oiled grill. Brush with lemon juice and butter. Cover and cook 5-6 minutes on each side.

To serve, place fish on heated platter. Stir sherry and chopped parsley into tomato sauce and spoon over fish. Sprinkle with grated parmesan and freshly grated black pepper. Serve with pasta.

Skewered Smelt

Whether you catch your own smelt or buy them frozen, they are a nice addition to your seafood diet. We have always enjoyed them rolled in cornmeal and fried the traditional way, but we were delighted when we tried them on the "barbie" in this easy kebab. Don't forget, the bones are edible, and when properly cooked they can be crunchy and a good source of calcium.

– R & W

1 lb	smelt, cleaned or thawed, if frozen	500 g
1	sweet pepper, cut in 1 1/2-inch (3.5-cm) squares	1
2	small zucchini, cut in 1/4-inch (5-mm) slices	2
12	cherry tomatoes	12
12	mushroom caps	12
3	slices bacon, cut in 4	3
1/4 cup	lemon juice	50 ml
1/4 cup	melted butter	50 ml
	salt and freshly ground black pepper	
1	lemon, cut in 4 wedges	1

Rinse smelt in cold water, place on paper towel, and pat dry. Cut in half lengthwise.

Thread the smelt onto oiled metal skewers, alternating the fish with the prepared vegetables and bacon pieces. Set aside.

Substitute shrimp or scallops, or salmon, halibut, or any other firm white fish cut into 1 1/2-inch (3.5-cm)cubes.

Preheat barbecue to medium-hot and place two bricks on grill.

In a small bowl, mix melted lemon juice and butter. Brush mixture over each prepared skewer, sprinkle with salt and pepper, and place skewers on bricks above grill. Cook for 10-12 minutes, turning once or twice and basting with lemon butter.

Garnish with lemon wedges and serve with hot steamed rice.

Barbecued Mackerel

SERVES 4-6

Mackerel is at its best when perfectly fresh, so try and cook it the day it is bought. Gut, leaving the mackerel heads and tails attached, and score the sides with three or four diagonal cuts. A light brushing of herbed oil will impart a unique, mellow flavour. Allow two fish per person, depending on appetites and the size of the mackerel.

– R & W

6	mackerel	6
	salt and freshly ground black pepper	
	herb or garlic oil	
	lemon wedges	

Preheat barbecue to medium-hot.

Lightly salt and pepper the inside of each mackerel. Using a garlic- or herb-infused oil, lightly brush the skin side of each fish and place them on the oiled grill. Close barbecue lid and grill about 5 minutes, until nicely browned. Turn, brush with oil and cook the other side for about 4 minutes. Serve hot off the grill with wedges of fresh lemon.

Just before the fish is cooked, brush on your favourite barbecue sauce. Turn once, brush again, and serve hot.

Sturgeon en Brochette

For years, giant sturgeon have been caught in the St. John River, on the east coast of Canada, and in the Fraser River, in the west. I remember when their roe was the only thing harvested, and the fish themselves were thrown away or used for mink or pig food. Times have changed: today, sturgeon is found on many fresh seafood counters and is worthy of your barbecue grill.
– R

2 Tbsp	butter	30 ml
1 Tbsp	canola oil	15 ml
2 Tbsp	lemon juice	30 ml
2 tsp	dried dill	10 ml
	or	
1 Tbsp	chopped fresh dill	15 ml
	paprika	
2 lb	sturgeon, cut in 2-inch (5-cm) cubes	1 kg

In a shallow glass baking dish, mix melted butter, oil, lemon juice, and dill. Place sturgeon in marinade, and turn well to coat. Let stand for 30 minutes. Soak bamboo skewers in cold water. Remove fish, reserving marinade. Thread chunks of sturgeon onto skewers.

Preheat barbecue to medium-hot, and place two bricks on grill.

Place skewers on bricks above grill and cook, covered, for 10 minutes, turning frequently and basting with marinade. Serve hot.

Swordfish with Salsa

SERVES 6

Swordfish is one of the most popular fish in North America and is found in temperate waters throughout the world. Available fresh from late spring until early fall, its firm, meat-like flesh is a natural for the barbecue.

– R & W

1/8 tsp	salt	.5 ml
1/8 tsp	coarsely ground black pepper	.5 ml
2 Tbsp	vegetable oil	30 ml
6	swordfish steaks, 1 inch (2.5 cm) thick	6
6	lemon or lime wedges	6

For the Salsa:

1	finely chopped onion	1
3	ripe tomatoes, peeled, seeded, and chopped	3
2 Tbsp	finely chopped cilantro	30 ml
1	garlic clove, minced	1
1	small green chili, seeded and minced	1
1 Tbsp	freshly squeezed lime or lemon juice	15 ml
	salt	

First prepare salsa. In a small bowl, combine all ingredients except salt, which should be added just before serving. Makes 3/4 cup (175 ml).

Preheat barbecue to hot.

In a small bowl, stir together salt, pepper, and oil. Brush on swordfish steaks, and place on oiled grill. Cover and cook them, basting with oil and turning occasionally, for 10-15 minutes, until fish flakes when prodded with fork. Garnish with lime or lemon wedges, and serve with salsa.

Leftover salsa can be refrigerated and served as a dip with tortilla chips.

Grilled Tuna Salad

SERVES 4

We often serve this grilled tuna with mashed potatoes and steamed vegetables, but it's superb on top of garden veggies, drizzled with vinaigrette.

– R & W

12	asparagus spears, cleaned and trimmed	12
2 cups	broccoli florets	500 ml
16-20	snow peas	16-20
3	peppers (red, yellow, and green) cut in strips	3
10	cherry tomatoes	10
4	6-oz (175-g) tuna steaks	4
	vegetable oil, for basting	

For the Vinaigrette:

1/2 cup	vegetable oil	125 ml
1/2 cup	olive oil	125 ml
1/4 cup	red wine vinegar	50 ml
1 Tbsp	balsamic vinegar	15 ml
2 tsp	grainy Dijon mustard	10 ml
1	garlic clove, minced	1
1/2 tsp	salt	2 ml
	freshly ground black pepper	

Preheat barbecue to hot.

In a large pot of boiling salted water, blanch asparagus, broccoli, and snow peas, then plunge them into ice water to cool. Drain and set aside with julienned peppers and tomatoes. Brush tuna steaks with vegetable oil, and grill 4-8 minutes per side, on oiled grill, with lid closed.

While fish is cooking, combine vinaigrette ingredients in a small bowl, and mix well. Taste and add additional salt and pepper if necessary. Makes about 1 1/4 cups (325 ml).

Arrange vegetables on individual plates, and place a tuna steak on each. Drizzle with vinaigrette, passing extra in a small pitcher.

Try using a flavoured olive oil in your vinaigrettes. Fruit-flavoured oils are especially good with fish.

Tuna Tingle

Fresh tuna is available in many fish markets. This spicy marinade will give your steaks a unique flavour.

— R & W

1/4 cup	finely chopped watercress	50 ml
1	spring onion, chopped	1
2	garlic cloves, diced	2
1/4 cup	canola oil	50 ml
3 Tbsp	dry sherry	45 ml
1 tsp	coarse salt	5 ml
	freshly ground black pepper	
4	8-oz (250-g) tuna steaks	4

Preheat grill to hot.

In a glass dish, combine watercress, spring onion, garlic, oil, sherry, and pepper. Add tuna, and marinate for 30-45 minutes, turning steaks once. Remove from marinade, sprinkle with salt, and sear on oiled, covered grill for 4-5 minutes on each side. Serve hot.

Ginger Shrimp Kebabs

SERVES 6

We find shrimp one of the fastest, tastiest foods to cook on the barbecue. Fresh or frozen, shrimp is versatile, too, and can be served as an appetizer or as a main course. Serve this tangy dish with steamed rice and lots of lemon wedges.

— R & W

24	medium or large shrimp	24
1	large red onion, cut in 12 wedges	1
12 oz	marinated artichoke hearts	350 g
2 tsp	grated fresh ginger	10 ml
1/2 tsp	salt	2 ml
1/2 tsp	freshly ground black pepper	2 ml
1/8 tsp	hot pepper sauce	.5 ml
1/2 tsp	minced garlic	2 ml
2 Tbsp	vegetable oil	30 ml
2	lemons, cut into wedges	2

[handwritten annotation: "overwhelming less" near red onion line]

Peel and devein fresh shrimp, leaving tail intact. Drain artichoke hearts, reserving 2 Tbsp (30 ml) of the marinade, and, if they're large, cut them in half. Thread shrimp, onion wedges, and artichoke hearts alternately on 6 oiled metal skewers. Set aside.

Preheat barbecue to medium-hot.

In a small bowl, mix reserved artichoke marinade with remaining ingredients except lemon. Brush kebabs with sauce, and place on metal skewer rack. Grill 5-7 minutes, basting and turning occasionally, until shrimp turn pink.

Serve with lemon wedges on a bed of rice.

Rolled Shrimp

SERVES 4–6

This makes an impressive and rather special appetizer. However, we also enjoy it with grilled vegetables and rice pilaf.

— R & W

24	large shrimp, shelled and deveined, with tails	24
12	spring onions, white parts only	12
12	bacon slices, cut in half	12
3 Tbsp	soy sauce	45 ml
3 Tbsp	sherry	45 ml
1/2 tsp	ground ginger	2 ml
1/2 tsp	ground nutmeg	2 ml
1/2 tsp	chili powder	2 ml
2	garlic cloves, chopped finely	2
2 Tbsp	brown sugar	30 ml

Carefully slice the shrimp along the inside curl, and open to form butterflies. Slice spring onions in half lengthwise, and place on open shrimp. Close up shrimp, and wrap each in a half-slice of bacon, securing with toothpick. Place in shallow glass baking dish.

In a small bowl, mix the remaining ingredients. Pour over shrimp. Marinate for at least 1 hour, turning occasionally.

Preheat barbecue to medium.

Place shrimp on oiled grill, and cook 6-7 minutes, until shrimp are firm and bacon is crispy.

Marinated Scallops with Summer Vegetables

SERVES 4

When our guests ask what they should order at a local seafood restaurant, we always recommend scallops. We know they'll never have them fresher than here in the Maritimes. We enjoy them whenever we can.

— R & W

6 Tbsp	olive oil	90 ml
3 Tbsp	lime juice	45 ml
1	garlic clove, chopped finely	1
2 Tbsp	chopped fresh basil	30 ml
	salt	
	freshly ground black pepper	
16	large fresh scallops	16
2	medium zucchini, cut in bite-sized chunks	2
1	eggplant, cut in bite-sized chunks	1
1	pepper, cut in bite-sized chunks	1
8	small mushrooms	8
	lime wedges, to garnish	

In a small bowl, mix olive oil and lime juice, and add garlic, basil, salt, and pepper. Add scallops, and marinate at room temperature for 30 minutes.

Preheat barbecue to medium-hot.

Reserve marinade. Thread scallops alternately with bite-sized veggies and mushrooms onto oiled metal skewers. Brush with marinade. Place skewers on rack over grill. Cook 8-10 minutes, turning occasionally and basting with marinade, until scallops are opaque. Serve with lime wedges.

Italian Scallops

10	slices prosciutto, cut in half	10
20	basil leaves	20
20	large scallops	20
	olive oil	
	lemon wedges	

Soak 10 bamboo skewers in water for 1 hour.

Place a basil leaf on top of a half-slice of prosciutto. Place a scallop on top of the leaf. Wrap the ham around the scallop, tucking in the sides to form a packet. Thread 2 wrapped scallops onto each bamboo skewer. Brush with olive oil.

Preheat barbecue to medium-hot, and place two bricks on grill.

Place skewers on bricks above grill. Cook in open barbecue 2-5 minutes per side, until prosciutto begins to brown. Serve with lemon wedges.

You can serve this delicious scallop dish as an appetizer or as the basis of a wonderful dinner. If serving as a main course, include Eggplant Stuffed Sweet Peppers (page 214), a bottle of red wine, and Foiled Poppyseed Loaf (page 225). Who could ask for more?

– R & W

Seafood Pizza

When you think about it, cooking pizza on the barbecue is not much different from using a gas oven. Although you can cook pizza right on the grill, a perforated pizza pan makes the job easier. Make your own pizza dough, or use frozen pizza shells.

You can sauté the onion in a pan or on aluminum foil set directly over your grill, and you can also grill the bacon slices.

– R & W

1	pizza crust	1
3 Tbsp	canola oil	45 ml
1/4 cup	tomato sauce	50 ml
1	onion, sliced and sautéed	1
3	slices bacon, cooked and diced	3
2	garlic cloves, chopped finely	2
1/2 lb	cooked salad shrimp	250 g
2	anchovy fillets, diced	2
1/4 lb	scallops, broken or sliced	125 g
1	green pepper, cut into thin rings	1
1 tsp	dried oregano	5 ml
1/2 cup	grated mozzarella cheese	125 ml
1/4 cup	crumbled goat's cheese	50 ml

Preheat barbecue to hot.

Place pizza crust on perforated pan, and brush lightly with oil. Spread tomato sauce on crust. Sprinkle with sautéed onion, bacon, garlic, shrimp, anchovies, and scallops. Add green pepper rings and sprinkle with oregano. Add grated mozzarella and dot with goat's cheese. Place on grill, cover, and cook for 15 minutes, until crust is brown and surface is hot and bubbling.

Lobster Zucchini Boats

SERVES 4 AS A MAIN COURSE
OR 8 AS AN APPETIZER

Zucchini's subtle flavour doesn't vie with the most important ingredient — lobster. You can, of course, substitute scallops, shrimp, or crab.

– R & W

4	10-inch (25-cm) zucchini	4
1/4 cup	dry bread crumbs	50 ml
1 Tbsp	melted butter	15 ml
1 lb	cooked lobster meat, chopped	500 g
1	egg, beaten lightly	1
2 Tbsp	mayonnaise	30 ml
2 tsp	lemon juice	10 ml
	dash of hot sauce	
1/4 cup	minced green onion	50 ml
1/4 cup	grated Swiss cheese	50 ml
1 Tbsp	grated parmesan cheese	15 ml
2 tsp	chopped fresh dill	10 ml
1/2 tsp	salt	2 ml
	freshly ground black pepper	
2 Tbsp	chopped fresh parsley	30 ml
1	lemon, cut into wedges	1

Cook whole zucchini in boiling salted water for 5 minutes. Remove and cool slightly. Halve lengthwise and scrape pulp from shells, reserving both pulp and shell.

In a small frying pan set over medium heat, melt butter and sauté bread crumbs, until browned. Set aside.

In a large bowl, combine chopped zucchini pulp with remaining ingredients, except lemon wedges. Fill zucchini shells with this mixture.

Preheat barbecue to medium-hot.

Place zucchini boats on oiled grill. Close lid and cook 10-15 minutes, until they begin to brown and bubble. Remove from barbecue, and sprinkle with bread crumbs. Halve to serve as an appetizer, or leave whole for a main course.

Crab Stuffed Mushrooms

SERVES 4-6

8 oz	chopped crab meat	250 g
4	water chestnuts, chopped finely	4
2 tsp	minced onion	10 ml
2 tsp	soy sauce	10 ml
1 tsp	sherry	5 ml
1 tsp	cornstarch	5 ml
1	egg yolk, beaten	1
1 Tbsp	whipping cream	15 ml
1 Tbsp	grated parmesan cheese	15 ml
12	large mushrooms	12
	chopped fresh parsley	

Stuffed mushrooms make a favourite appetizer, and this recipe can be prepared ahead, giving you more time to spend with your guests. Lobster makes a great substitute.

– R & W

In a large bowl, combine crab meat, chestnuts, onion, soy sauce, sherry, cornstarch, egg yolk, cream, and parmesan. Trim the mushrooms, mincing the stems and sautéing quickly for 2-3 minutes. Add to mixture. Set aside.

Preheat barbecue to hot.

Brush mushroom caps with oil and place on oiled grill, stem-side down. Cook 3-5 minutes, until lightly browned. Remove from grill and stuff with crab mixture. Return to grill, stuffing-side up, and cook 3-5 minutes, until filling is heated and mushrooms are golden brown.

Sprinkle with chopped parsley, and serve at once.

Barbecued Oysters

When buying oysters in the shell, ask if they're freshly harvested, and make sure all the shells are closed tightly. Discard any that are open and don't close when handled.

– R & W

24	oysters, live in shells	24
2	lemons, cut in wedges	2
	Worcestershire Sauce	
	freshly ground black pepper	

Heat barbecue to medium-hot.

Rinse any sand or grit from oysters. Set oysters on the grill, placing them so the bottom (cupped) shell lies flat and will hold the oyster when cooked. Close the lid and cook for 6-7 minutes, until oysters pop open. As they open, carefully remove them, using tongs or oven mitts. Place oysters on a platter, and surround with lemon wedges. Have the pepper mill and Worcestershire Sauce handy for those who might want them. Once the shells have cooled sufficiently, squeeze on some lemon juice, and suck the oysters and their heavenly nectar right from the shells.

Bacon Wrapped Oysters

SERVES 6

24	small mushrooms, cleaned	24
1/2 cup	butter	125 ml
	juice and zest of 1 lemon	
1/4 cup	chopped fresh parsley	50 ml
	pinch of cayenne pepper	
24	fresh oysters, shelled	24
	cornstarch	
12	slices lean bacon	12
	lemon wedges	

This delicious appetizer or first course can be served on toast or presented in a clean oyster shell, drizzled with a bit of lemon butter.

– R & W

In a small pan of boiling water, blanch mushrooms for 1 minute. Drain and set aside. Use the same pan to melt butter. Remove from heat and add lemon juice, 1 tsp (5 ml) zest, parsley, and cayenne pepper. Set aside and keep warm.

Preheat barbecue to medium-hot.

Dust oysters with cornstarch by shaking them, a few at a time, in a small paper bag with the cornstarch. Cut bacon slices in half, and wrap around oysters, securing with toothpicks. Alternate wrapped oysters with mushrooms on oiled metal skewers, and brush with lemon butter. Barbecue on skewer rack set over grill for 3-4 minutes, until bacon begins to brown. Turn and cook the other side. Remove from skewers, and serve immediately with lemon wedges.

Shellfish Skewers

If you're counting calories, reserve the pineapple juice. Omit the butter, and use the pineapple juice to baste the skewers. If you're only half-heartedly counting calories, use half butter and half pineapple juice.

This non-traditional method for cooking oysters works well, and the oysters are terrific served on a bed of fragrant rice. If you have difficulty shucking fresh oysters, ask your fishmonger to shuck them for you. Often you will find them ready-shucked in half-pint containers. It doesn't alter their flavour at all, and it saves your bruised fingers.

– R & W

24	fresh oysters, shucked	24
24	medium scallops	24
14 oz	can pineapple chunks	398 ml
1	red pepper, cut in 1-inch (2.5-cm) chunks	1
2	small zucchini, cut in 1-inch (2.5-cm) chunks	2
	melted butter	
	freshly ground black pepper	
	lemon wedges	

Drain oysters and pat dry. Thread oysters, scallops, pineapple chunks, red pepper chunks, and zucchini chunks alternately onto oiled metal skewers. Brush with butter and sprinkle with pepper.

Preheat barbecue to medium-hot.

Place skewers on skewer rack, and grill about 7 minutes, basting with butter and turning occasionally, until seafood begins to brown. Serve with lemon wedges.

BEEF

The days are long gone when massive slabs of beef overpowered tiny charcoal- or gas-fired grills. Today the emphasis is on quality-rather-than-quantity dining. Health-conscious diners now prefer leaner cuts of beef, and care must be taken when cooking these that they do not dry out. High-grade beef usually comes from cattle weighing between 900 and 1300 pounds (400-600 kg). Most cuts of meat that are taken from working, muscular sections of the animal, such as legs, hips and shoulders, are less tender than cuts taken from supporting sections, such as ribs and loins. Streaks of fat, called marbling, help make beef moist, flavourful and tender. The extent of the marbling varies with the cut as well as with the grade of beef. Loin, rib, and chuck cuts should be well marbled.

Cuts of beef that are less expensive, such as those from the chuck (the top front shoulder), are best marinated in mixtures of oil and acidic fruit juices or vinegars to help tenderize them and impart flavour. Longer cooking is also necessary for chuck or blade steaks and pot roasts.

The more expensive rib and short loin cuts, including standing rib and prime rib roasts and porterhouse, T-bone, and club steaks, don't need marinating, as they are tender and flavourful as is. These roast or grill well at higher temperatures and in a shorter amount of time. Standing rib and rolled rib roasts are best for rotisserie cooking. The fat within these cuts and around the exterior of the roasts bastes the meat as it turns over the heat. The lower portions of the rib and short loin section produce short ribs, plate, and flank cuts. These need slow grilling or braising in a closed container or foil packet, with the addition of water, fruit juice, or wine.

The upper portion, between the sirloin and short loin, is where the tenderloin is found. Filet mignon, from the small end of the tenderloin, is unquestionably the most tender cut of beef. These cuts require little cooking time at medium to high temperature.

Ground beef for hamburgers and round steak cuts for slow, moist cooking are primarily from the round portion of the hind leg. Hamburger or ground beef can be purchased in at least three grades: lean contains 17% fat, medium has 23% fat, and regular has 30% fat per pound. While it's common to think that leaner is better, remember that the leaner grades can dry out with too much cooking.

To destroy any harmful bacteria, all ground beef must be cooked to an internal temperature of 160°F (70°C), or until no pink remains. I prefer other cuts of beef cooked somewhere between medium-rare and medium; for me, beef cooked to about 155°F (68°C) is more flavourful and juicy than well-done beef. That said, cooking is about personal preference — if you like your beef well done, by all means cook it that way.

Beef can be cooked in many different ways. The largest roast I ever cooked was a 40-pound boneless hip of beef on a hand-turned spit over a charcoal fire. It was a labour of love but well worth the nine hours of effort.

—R

Beef Pit Barbecue

I recommend trying this when you have a couple of muscular friends on hand to help with the hard work, and a crowd of deserving friends to join in the feast.

– R

Dig a hole 3 feett (1 m) around and 3 feet (1 m) deep. Line it with rocks, and build a large fire in it. Keep the fire burning well for 3 hours, and then let it die down to reveal hot coals and embers.

Wrap each of two large (10-lb/4.5-kg) beef roasts in a layer of aluminum foil and several layers of wet burlap sacking, and tie the parcels securely together with soft iron wire. Have a large piece of sheet metal on hand, big enough to cover the firepit completely. With the help of a friend, quickly drop the wrapped roasts into the pit of glowing embers, and cover it immediately with the sheet metal.

Shovel earth as quickly as possible over the top. This all has to be done rapidly to seal the pit, as access to air will cause the meat to incinerate. After you've covered the pit with earth to a depth of 5-6 inches (13-15 cm), watch for steam. Shovel more earth on any spot from which steam is escaping. Once all is secure, head into the house, and get ready for the party some 6 hours later.

The nerve-wracking part is when your guests gather, plates and appetites in hand. Shovel the earth off the sheet metal, remove it with gloved hands, and lift the charcoal-black bundles from the earthen oven. The aroma of roast beef should be overwhelmingly gratifying. Cut the wire, and remove the burlap layers and aluminum foil to reveal the succulent, tender meat. Your guests will enjoy the unique way in which their dinner was cooked and hold a new respect for the chef's courage.

Beef Tenderloin

SERVES 8

The tenderloin or filet is the most expensive cut of beef. But, as its name implies, it is also the most tender. We like it for barbecuing because it cooks beautifully, becoming charred on the outside while staying juicy on the inside. Most people are eating much smaller helpings of meat these days, so it isn't that extravagant to serve the best now and then. Enjoy this with Yorkshire Puddings (page 46) and Béarnaise Sauce (page 229).

– R & W

4-5 lb	beef tenderloin	2-2.5 kg
	vegetable oil	
	freshly ground black pepper	

Use an instant thermometer to test meat on the barbecue. Insert it into the thickest portion of the meat, avoiding any bone or gristle, toward the end of the cooking time. It will give you the internal temperature of the meat in just a few seconds.

Preheat barbecue to hot.

Tenderloin is generally thick at one end, tapering at the other. Cooked as is, it will provide you with a fine selection of meat, from rare to well done. Or you can fold the tapered end in on itself and secure it with toothpicks, which will render the tenderloin more uniform in size and degree of doneness.

Either way, brush the meat with oil, and place it on a well-oiled grill. Sear for 2 minutes, then turn and sear the other side for 2 minutes. Reduce heat to medium, close the barbecue cover, and cook, turning frequently, 10 minutes per side for rare meat, or until the meat thermometer reads 120°F (50°C).

Remove from grill, and cover loosely with foil. Leave for 5 minutes before carving, to allow juices to set. Carve into 3/4-inch (1.5-cm) slices, and serve hot or cold.

Stuffed Burgundy Steak

SERVES 4-6

There was a time when I would sit down to a 1-lb (500-g) porter-house and eat it all. I was 19 years old, an avid downhill skier, walker, and climber. Today, this recipe is more my speed.

– W

2 lb	porterhouse steak	1 kg
1 Tbsp	butter	15 ml
2 tsp	finely chopped garlic	10 ml
1/2 cup	chopped onion	125 ml
1/2 cup	chopped mushrooms	125 ml
	salt and freshly ground black pepper	
1/4 cup	burgundy or other hearty red wine	50 ml
2 Tbsp	soy sauce	30 ml

Using a sharp knife, make a series of cuts, every inch (2.5 cm) or so, along the fatty edge of the steak. Then create a pocket along the same fat side, cutting into the meat almost to the bone. Set aside. Soak several toothpicks in water.

Melt butter in a small frying pan over medium heat, and sauté garlic, onion and mushrooms. Season with salt and pepper. Remove from heat. With a spoon, stuff mixture into steak pocket. Use toothpicks to secure pocket.

Preheat barbecue to medium-hot.

Mix wine and soy sauce, and brush over steak. Place steak on oiled grill, cover, and cook 25-30 minutes, turning once and brushing occasionally with wine and soy sauce. Remove when cooked to your liking.

Leave 5 minutes, and then slice steak across the grain.

Lobster Stuffed Steak

1 lb	cooked lobster meat	500 g
2 tsp	lemon juice	10 ml
4	1 1/2-inch (3.5-cm) thick filet steaks	4
2 Tbsp	melted butter	30 ml
1 Tbsp	chopped fresh parsley	15 ml
	HP or other steak sauce	
1	lemon, cut in 4 wedges	1

This recipes is a wonderful union of land and sea.
– R & W

Preheat barbecue to medium-hot. Soak 8 toothpicks in water.

In a medium-sized bowl, combine lobster and lemon juice. Cut a small pocket in the side of each steak. Fill pockets with lobster, securing openings with toothpicks. In a small bowl, combine melted butter and chopped parsley.

Brush steaks with melted butter. Place on oiled barbecue, and cook 6-8 minutes on each side, basting frequently with melted butter.

Remove toothpicks before serving steaks with HP Sauce (or other steak sauce), lemon wedges, and Baked Potatoes with Garlic Cream (page 206).

Steak with Creamy Horseradish

SERVES 4

We have given roots of this invasive plant growing at the end of our garden to several people. Look for this pungent root at roadside vegetable stands, or buy grated horseradish bottled at the supermarket.

– W

6 Tbsp	grated horseradish	90 ml
1/4 cup	apple cider vinegar	50 ml
3 Tbsp	vegetable oil	45 ml
2 lb	sirloin steak, cut in 4 pieces	1 kg
1 cup	sour cream	250 ml
1/2 tsp	salt	2 ml
	freshly ground black pepper	

In a small bowl, mix half the horseradish with vinegar and vegetable oil. Place steak in shallow glass baking dish, and pour the oil mixture over it, turning to coat well. Cover and refrigerate for 8 hours or overnight, turning occasionally.

In a small bowl, mix sour cream, remaining horseradish, salt, and pepper. Cover and refrigerate.

Preheat barbecue to hot.

Remove steak, reserving marinade, and place on oiled grill. Cook, turning and basting occasionally with marinade, for 10-15 minutes for medium, less time for rare, more for well done.

Serve with creamy horseradish sauce.

Cranberry Glazed Short Ribs

SERVES 4-6

4	garlic cloves, halved	4
6 lb	short ribs, in serving-sized pieces	3 kg
1 tsp	salt	5 ml
1 tsp	freshly ground black pepper	5 ml
2 cups	cranberries, fresh or frozen	500 ml
3/4 cup	sugar	175 ml
1/3 cup	apple cider vinegar	75 ml
1/4 cup	tomato ketchup	50 ml

Short ribs do very well on the grill when precooked in a microwave, Dutch oven, or pressure cooker. Precooking the ribs ensures juicy tenderness and a greatly reduced fat content. These ribs are still quite rich, and the piquant cranberry glaze makes an ideal foil.

– R & W

Rub cut garlic cloves all over ribs. Sprinkle ribs with salt and pepper, and place in a pot with 1 cup (250 ml) water and garlic cloves. Cover and simmer for 2 hours, until meat is fairly tender. Check occasionally, adding more water if necessary.

In a small pan over medium heat, combine cranberries, sugar, and vinegar. Bring to a boil, and simmer until berries pop and soften. Add ketchup and stir well, thinning with a little water if necessary. Set aside.

Preheat barbecue to hot.

Drain ribs, and cover with cranberry sauce, turning to coat well. Place on oiled grill. Cook, turning frequently and basting with glaze, making sure they don't burn. When ribs are hot and sizzling, serve at once.

Curried Short Ribs

A neighbour who had four sons introduced me to short ribs about 25 years ago. He bought them because they were a delicious and inexpensive way to feed a large family. They're no longer inexpensive, but they're still tasty.

– W

4 lb	short ribs, in serving-sized pieces	2 kg
	salt and freshly ground black pepper	
2/3 cup	tomato ketchup	150 ml
1/4 cup	molasses	50 ml
1/4 cup	lemon juice	50 ml
1 Tbsp	dry mustard	15 ml
1/2 tsp	curry powder	2 ml
	pinch of garlic powder	

Trim fat from ribs. Sprinkle with salt and pepper, and place in a large, heavy pan. Add water to cover. Cover and simmer about 2 hours, until meat is tender. Drain.

Preheat barbecue to hot.

In a bowl, mix ketchup, molasses, lemon juice, mustard, curry, and garlic powder. Brush on ribs, and place on oiled grill. Cook, turning frequently and basting with sauce. When ribs are hot and sizzling, serve at once.

London Broil

2 lb	flank steak	1 kg
1 cup	vegetable oil	250 ml
1 3/4 cups	dry red wine	425 ml
4 Tbsp	soy sauce	60 ml
4 tsp	chopped fresh parsley	20 ml
1	garlic clove, minced	1
1 tsp	salt	5 ml
	freshly ground black pepper	
1 Tbsp	finely chopped onion	15 ml
1/2 cup	softened butter	125 ml

London Broil is made from flank steak tenderized by marinating, cooked briefly, and sliced thinly across the grain. It's a wonderful way to serve what was once considered an undesirable cut of beef. Have your butcher save you a flank steak the next time you're expecting company.
– R & W

Trim excess fat from steak, and score on both sides, using a sharp knife. In a glass baking dish, combine oil, 1 cup (250 ml) wine, soy sauce, 2 tsp (10 ml) parsley, garlic, salt, and pepper. Add steak. Leave at room temperature for 4 hours, or refrigerate overnight, turning several times.

Combine chopped onion with remaining wine in a small saucepan over medium heat. Cook until reduced to 1/4 cup (50 ml). Remove from heat and cool.

In a small bowl, cream butter with remaining parsley, and gradually whisk in wine mixture until creamy and smooth. Season to taste with salt and pepper.

Preheat barbecue to hot.

Place steak on lightly oiled grill, and cook 4-5 minutes. Baste with marinade, turn, and cook 4-5 minutes longer, until medium-rare. Remove to cutting board, and slice thinly on the diagonal across the grain. Serve with wine sauce.

Skewered Sirloin

*We once devoted an entire episode of our television cooking show,
Tide's Table, to cooking with beer. Beer can be substituted for milk
when making bread, for water in a pot roast, or for wine or vinegar
in a marinade, as we have done here.*

– R & W

1 1/2 cups	beer	375 ml
1/4 cup	diced onion	50 ml
2 Tbsp	vegetable oil	30 ml
1 tsp	salt	5 ml
1 tsp	chili powder	5 ml
1/2 tsp	Worcestershire Sauce	2 ml
1	garlic clove, crushed	1
1 lb	boneless sirloin, cut in cubes	500 g
16	button mushrooms	16
1	green pepper, cut in chunks	1

In a shallow glass baking dish, combine beer, onion, oil, salt, chili
powder, Worcestershire Sauce, and garlic. Add beef and marinate 3-4
hours at room temperature.

Preheat barbecue to hot.

Drain beef, reserving marinade. Thread meat onto 4 oiled metal
skewers, alternating with mushrooms and pepper pieces. Place on
skewer rack on grill, and cook 7-8 minutes, brushing frequently with
marinade. Turn, cooking 3-4 minutes more, until cooked to your liking.

Filet Mignon Stroganoff

SERVES 4

When we first created this recipe, Ross compared it to paving the driveway with diamonds. However, we like stroganoff and it was an interesting challenge to make it on the barbecue. We also wanted to experiment with filet mignon, because now we enjoy smaller portions of steak. I like this served on a bed of fresh egg noodles.

– W

Medium-rare meat will be slightly soft when pressed with your fingertips, medium meat will be springy, and well-done meat should be firm.

1 Tbsp	butter	15 ml
1	garlic clove, minced	1
1/4 lb	mushrooms, sliced	125 g
1	small carrot, diced finely	1
1	green onion, minced	1
1 tsp	paprika	5 ml
1/2 tsp	salt	2 ml
1 cup	sour cream	250 ml
1 tsp	Worcestershire Sauce	5 ml
	dash of Tabasco Sauce	
4	filets, 1 1/4 inch (3 cm) thick	4
	vegetable oil	

Preheat barbecue to hot.

Melt butter in a large frying pan over medium heat. Sauté garlic for 3 minutes, and then add mushrooms, carrot and onion. Lower heat, and season vegetables with paprika and salt. Stir in sour cream and Worcestershire and Tabasco sauces. Mix well, and heat through for about 2 minutes, being careful not to curdle the sauce. Keep warm over low heat while you grill the steaks.

Rub steaks with vegetable oil, and place on oiled grill, cooking 2-3 minutes on each side for rare, or to your own taste. Pour sauce over steaks and serve at once.

Grandma's Pot Roast

SERVES 6-8

3-4 lb	boneless rump roast	2 kg
6	medium-sized potatoes, quartered	6
2 cups	carrots, cut in large pieces	500 ml
2	onions, quartered	2
19 oz	can Italian-style stewed tomatoes, undrained	540 ml
1	envelope onion soup mix	1
3 Tbsp	flour	45 ml
1/4 tsp	freshly ground black pepper	1 ml

When Grandma visits, we like to serve something special, bearing in mind that she isn't truly happy unless she has potatoes. She no longer cooks roasts for herself, and we often make enough for her to take home leftovers to reheat in the microwave. We like to cook this favourite in a foil cooking bag.
– R & W

Preheat grill to medium.

Open the foil bag and place in shallow baking pan. (Alternatively, use a large sheet of heavy-duty aluminum foil.) Add roast, arranging vegetables around meat. Combine remaining ingredients, and spoon over roast and vegetables. Seal bag by double-folding open end. (If using aluminum foil, turn sides up to form envelope, and seal by making double folds on top and sides.)

Carefully slide foil packet onto grill. Cover and cook 1 1/2 hours. Remove from grill, using oven mitts. Pierce foil to let steam escape. Allow to set for 5 minutes. Place roast on cutting board, slice, and serve with vegetables and juices.

Hot Thyme Veal Chops

Whenever we see veal in our market, we buy it with our barbecue in mind. It's easy to vary the flavour by changing the herbs, but thyme is always our first choice.

– R & W

4	1-inch (2.5-cm) veal chops	4
	olive oil	
	salt	
	freshly ground black pepper	
1/4 cup	softened butter	50 ml
2 tsp	dry mustard	10 ml
2 Tbsp	chopped fresh thyme	30 ml
1 tsp	lemon zest	5 ml

Preheat barbecue to hot.

Brush chops with olive oil and place on well-oiled grill. Close barbecue lid, and cook 4 minutes. Brush again with oil, sprinkle with salt and pepper, turn and cook 3-4 minutes, or to your taste.

Meanwhile, in a small bowl, blend butter, mustard, thyme, and lemon zest. Put a spoonful of butter on each cooked chop, and serve at once.

Steak Sandwich Mexicana

SERVES 4

Both Ross and Greg, my son, love a steak sandwich, frequently ordering one when we eat lunch in a restaurant. This is the one I order when we eat in.

– W

1 lb	1-inch (2.5-cm) sirloin steak	500 g
	vegetable oil	
3 Tbsp	butter	45 ml
1	large onion, chopped	1
2	peppers (green and red), seeded and chopped	2
2 Tbsp	tomato paste	30 ml
1/2 cup	hot beef bouillon	125 ml
1/2 tsp	salt	2 ml
	freshly ground black pepper	
	dash Tabasco Sauce	
4	kaiser rolls or thick slices French bread	4
1/2 tsp	finely minced garlic	2 ml

Preheat barbecue to hot.

Melt 1 Tbsp (15 ml) butter in a large frying pan over medium heat. Sauté onion and peppers for 5 minutes, until softened. Stir in tomato paste, bouillon, salt, pepper, and Tabasco Sauce. Simmer 10 minutes.

Trim fat from steaks. Using tongs, rub grill with trimmings. Brush steak with oil, and grill for 4 minutes. Turn and cook 4 minutes more.

In a small bowl, cream remaining butter with garlic and salt. Spread on split kaiser rolls or bread, and place, buttered side down, on grill. Toast lightly, remove from grill, and place on individual warmed plates. Slice steak thinly on the diagonal, and divide between roll halves or bread. Spoon sauce over top, and serve any remaining sauce on the side.

Calves' Liver with Bacon and Red Onions

SERVES 4

Liver and onions is a Maritime favourite, so why not enjoy it cooked on the barbecue? We have to serve it at least once each summer.

– R & W

1 1/2 lb	calves' liver, 1/2 inch (1 cm) thick	750 g
1	large red onion, cut in 1/2-inch (1-cm) slices	1
3 Tbsp	melted butter	45 ml
	freshly ground black pepper	
	salt	
8	slices bacon	8

Preheat barbecue to medium-hot.

Remove membrane and cut liver in 4 pieces.

Place onion slices in wire basket, or keep from falling apart with toothpicks (page 213). Brush with melted butter, cook on oiled grill for 5 minutes, turn, season with pepper, and cook for 5 minutes more. Meanwhile, brush liver with melted butter, grill 2-3 minutes, then turn, baste again, and cook 2-3 minutes more. At the same time, grill bacon slices until crisp.

Serve on individual plates, placing a piece of liver on 2 strips of bacon, and top with an onion slice.

Grilled Pastrami and Onion Sandwiches

SERVES 4

Hot sandwiches take on a whole new meaning when you prepare them on the grill. Even Willa, who eats sandwiches only as a last resort, enjoys these.

– R

1 cup	thinly sliced red onion	250 ml
1 cup	thinly sliced Spanish or Vidalia onion	250 ml
2 Tbsp	maple syrup	30 ml
1 Tbsp	grainy Dijon mustard	15 ml
1 Tbsp	apple cider vinegar	15 ml
2 Tbsp	butter or margarine	30 ml
8	thick slices French bread	8
1/2 lb	pastrami, sliced	250 g
8	slices Swiss cheese	8
	dill pickles	

Preheat barbecue to medium.

In a large saucepan, combine onions, maple syrup, mustard, and vinegar. Cook over medium heat 2-3 minutes, stirring occasionally, until onions are just tender.

Lightly butter bread on one side. Top the unbuttered side of 4 slices with pastrami, onions, and Swiss cheese. Place second slice of bread on top, butter side out. Grill, turning occasionally, 10-12 minutes, or until cheese is melted and bread is toasted. Serve with crisp dill pickles.

Old Faithful Beef Burgers

SERVES 4

1	egg, beaten lightly	1
1 lb	medium ground beef	500 g
1 Tbsp	milk or water	15 ml
1/4 cup	bread crumbs	50 ml
1 tsp	Worcestershire Sauce	5 ml
	salt and freshly ground black pepper	
4	hamburger buns	4

Preheat grill to medium-hot.

In a large mixing bowl, combine egg, beef, milk or water, and bread crumbs. Mix well, and season with Worcestershire Sauce and salt and pepper. Form into 4 patties about 3/4 inch (2 cm) thick. Grill for 10-12 minutes, turning once. Serve on toasted buns, offering an assortment of "old faithful" condiments.

These burgers have nothing to do with the famous geyser in Yellowstone National Park but everything to do with taste and flavour. When it comes to beef burgers, Willa and I believe the flavour of good beef should be foremost. Guests can exercise their individual tastes and "doctor up" their burgers as desired. One bite and you'll know it's your "Old Faithful Burger."

– R

Matterhorn Burgers

For more sophisticated palates, add pâté to the burgers; it acts as a binder and imparts its own flavour. Sauerkraut and Swiss cheese add a European tang.

– R & W

1 lb	ground beef	500 g
4 oz	liver pâté	125 g
1/4 cup	finely chopped onion	50 ml
1/2 tsp	freshly minced garlic	2 ml
1/4 tsp	salt	1 ml
	dash hot sauce	
1/4 lb	Swiss cheese, sliced thinly	125 g
1/2 lb	sauerkraut, drained	250 g
4	hamburger buns	4

Preheat barbecue to medium.

In a large bowl, mix beef, pâté, onion, garlic, salt, and hot sauce. Shape into 4 patties. Cook on oiled grill 10-12 minutes, turning once. Just before serving, toast buns, and serve each with a beef patty topped with cheese and sauerkraut.

Mushroom Meat Loaf Burgers

SERVES 4-6

1 lb	ground beef	500 g
2 Tbsp	finely chopped onion	30 ml
1	egg, beaten	1
2 Tbsp	milk	30 ml
2 Tbsp	tomato ketchup	30 ml
1/3 cup	bread or cracker crumbs	75 ml
1 Tbsp	Worcestershire Sauce	15 ml
	dash garlic powder	
1 tsp	salt	5 ml
1/4 tsp	freshly ground black pepper	1 ml
4-6	hamburger buns	4-6

When we're rushed at the Inn, we often barbecue hamburgers to free the kitchen to prepare a reception. These are juicy and special.

– W

For the Mushroom Topping:

2 Tbsp	butter or margarine	30 ml
1/2 lb	mushrooms, sliced	250 g
1/4 cup	chopped green onions, with tops	50 ml
1 Tbsp	chopped fresh parsley	15 ml
1/4 tsp	salt	1 ml
1/4 tsp	Worcestershire Sauce	1 ml

Chilling hamburger patties will help them to hold their shape when grilled. You can also freeze them in stacks, divided by sheets of waxed paper. Thaw in the refrigerator before grilling.

In a large bowl, mix all the burger ingredients. Shape into 4 large or 6 medium patties. Refrigerate for at least 1 hour.

To prepare topping, melt butter in a frying pan. Sauté mushrooms, onions, and parsley, until tender. Stir in salt and Worcestershire Sauce, lower heat, and keep warm.

Preheat barbecue to hot.

Place patties on oiled grill, and cook 6 minutes on each side, or to your liking. Toast buns on grill, and serve with mushroom topping.

Bacon Wrapped Meat Loaf

SERVES 6-8

1 lb	medium ground beef	500 g
1 lb	ground pork	500 g
2	eggs, beaten	2
1/2 cup	chopped onion	125 ml
1 tsp	salt	5 ml
1 Tbsp	chopped fresh parsley	15 ml
2 Tbsp	Worcestershire Sauce	30 ml
1 tsp	dry mustard	5 ml
1/4 cup	tomato ketchup	50 ml
1/2 cup	applesauce	125 ml
2 cups	bread or cracker crumbs	500 ml
1/4 tsp	poultry seasoning or dry sage	1 ml
6-8	bacon strips	6-8

After we tried cooking roast beef and Yorkshire Pudding on the barbecue (page 229), we decided to experiment with another of our favourites — meat loaf. Much to our delight, it turned out beautifully. Serve with baked potatoes and your favourite salad.

– R & W

Preheat barbecue to medium.

In a large bowl, mix together everything except bacon. Shape into a loaf, and wrap bacon strips around it, securing with toothpicks, until loaf is completely covered.

Place loaf directly on oiled grill. Cover and cook for 1 1/2 hours, turning regularly, until done. To test, insert a skewer into centre of loaf. If juices run clear, loaf is cooked. Remove from heat, and let sit for 10 minutes. Slice and serve.

Beef Jerky

Beef Jerky requires a low, slow-cooking barbecue, and for this reason, gas or electric barbecues work best because they require less tending than charcoal. As with other smoked products, brining the meat beforehand is essential. A word of advice: It takes a lot longer to prepare Beef Jerky than it does to eat it! We often made this dried meat for backpacking and canoe trips. It can be chewed for a long time and will develop great flavour.

– R

5 lb	lean beef steak or roast	2.5 kg
1 quart	cold water	1 litre
1/3 cup	non-iodized pickling salt	75 ml
1/2 cup	brown sugar	125 ml
1 Tbsp	molasses	15 ml
1/4 cup	soy sauce	50 ml
1 tsp	freshly ground black pepper	5 ml
1	bay leaf	1
2	garlic cloves, chopped	2
1 Tbsp	Worcestershire Sauce	15 ml

Trim all fat from meat, and place it in the freezer for about 1 hour to firm it up by partially freezing it. Using a sharp knife or circular electric slicer, slice meat with the grain, as thinly as possible. In a large plastic bucket, glass bowl, or pottery crock, combine water, salt, sugar, molasses, soy sauce, pepper, bay leaf, garlic, and Worcestershire Sauce, stirring well. Place sliced meat in brine, and refrigerate overnight. After 12 hours, remove meat from brine, and let pieces air-dry on wire racks for about 1 hour.

Preheat barbecue to lowest setting.

Place two bricks on one grill, and put the other grill on top of the bricks to elevate it well above briquettes and flames. Place a metal pie plate filled with alder, maple, or apple wood chips alongside the bricks. Carefully place the wire racks with the jerky on them on the top grill, and close the lid. Smoke will develop shortly. Leave the meat to cook and smoke for 4 hours, then refill the pan with wood chips. Continue smoking for 6 hours more, or until the meat is dry and quite firm. Then remove the wood chips, and cook until the meat is fully dry. Transfer the meat to a glass jar with holes punched in the lid, and refrigerate.

LAMB

Lamb is perfect for the barbecue, delectable and quick to cook. More than 90% of all fresh meat from sheep consumed in North America is lamb. Young sheep of either sex that have not reached maturity can be marketed as lamb. Mutton, from mature sheep more than 20 months old, has a much stronger flavour than its younger counterpart and is seldom eaten here.

The colour of lean lamb tends to become darker with age: the pinker the flesh, the younger the animal. A fine, velvety texture is preferred, with the fat firm, white, somewhat brittle, but waxy. A tough parchment-like covering of exterior fat can be removed with a sharp knife before cooking, if you wish. The jury is still out on whether the removal of this covering, called "fell," makes any difference to the flavour, cooking, or tenderness. Marinades will penetrate lamb more easily, however, if the fell has been removed.

Prime cuts of lamb for grilling are the rib and loin chops. Leg of lamb and rolled shoulder roasts are best when cooked on the rotisserie. If ground lamb is not readily available, ask your butcher to grind some flank, breast, or shank meat; it is a delicious alternative to hamburger.

Stuffed Lamb Roast

SERVES 4-6

The aroma of roasting lamb beckons like the "sirens of the sea" that lured ancient Greek mariners onto the rocks. Be sure to have a tall glass of Sangria on the rocks (page 234) ready for your guests when they are drawn irresistibly to your grill as the fragrance of this roast lamb wafts on the breeze.

– R & W

3-4 lb	leg of lamb, boned	1.5-2 kg
2 Tbsp	olive oil	30 ml
1	small onion, chopped	1
2	garlic cloves, chopped finely	2
6 oz	spinach, chopped coarsely	175 g
2 Tbsp	lemon juice	30 ml
1 Tbsp	chopped fresh oregano	15 ml
2 Tbsp	tomato paste	30 ml
1 tsp	dried basil	5 ml
1 tsp	cardamom	5 ml
1/4 cup	bread crumbs	50 ml
	extra olive oil and lemon juice, for basting	

Preheat barbecue to medium.

In a skillet set over medium-high heat, heat oil and sauté onion for 5 minutes. Stir in garlic and spinach. Add lemon juice, oregano, tomato paste, basil, and cardamom. Stir to mix, cover, and cook 2 minutes. Remove from heat. Add bread crumbs and mix well. Let cool slightly.

Lay boned leg of lamb open, skin-side down. Spoon stuffing mixture along its length, roll meat closed, and tie tightly into a roll, using strong butcher cord or string. Secure on spit in the usual fashion, or use a spit basket to hold roast securely. Place a drip pan containing 1 cup (250 ml) of water on the grill under the roast. Close barbecue lid, and cook for 1 1/2 - 2 hours, basting occasionally with oil and lemon juice.

Lamb Cyprus Style

SERVES 6

While visiting the island of Cyprus many years ago, I was overwhelmed by the number of succulent lamb dishes available. Lamb was often roasted according to this recipe outside homes on feast days. Serve on a bed of steamed rice with a pile of grilled vegetables.

– R

3 lb	leg of lamb, boned	1.5 kg
1 cup	dry white wine	250 ml
3/4 cup	olive oil	175 ml
1/2 cup	lemon juice	125 ml
1	large onion, diced finely	1
1	stalk celery, diced finely	1
1	sprig fresh thyme	1
1	fresh bay leaf	1
1	tomato, diced finely	1

Cut lamb in 6 or 8 large pieces. In a large glass bowl, mix remaining ingredients. Put lamb into marinade, and turn to coat well. Leave at room temperature 3-4 hours.

Preheat barbecue to medium-hot.

Thread lamb chunks onto motorized spit, and secure well with forks and twine or iron wire, if necessary. Cook slowly over drip pan for 40-60 minutes, basting frequently with marinade.

Piquant Leg of Lamb

Friends of ours often run out of grass in the summer, so we "sheep sit" for them. Our guests are always reassured when we tell them these are wool sheep, and in these weeks there's no lamb on the menu.
– R & W

5 lb	leg of lamb	2.5 kg
	vegetable oil	
	salt and freshly ground black pepper	
1/2 cup	water	125 ml
1/2 cup	red wine	125 ml
1 Tbsp	Worcestershire Sauce	15 ml
1/4 cup	lemon juice	50 ml
1 tsp	dry mustard	5 ml
	dash Tabasco Sauce	
1/4 tsp	paprika	1 ml
1	garlic clove, chopped	1
1	onion, grated	1

Preheat barbecue to low.

Rub lamb with vegetable oil, salt, and pepper. Place on grill, cover, and cook 45-60 minutes. Turn occasionally, and brush with oil. Watch carefully — if lamb appears to be burning or browning too quickly, turn one side of the grill off, and move lamb to that side.

In a medium-sized saucepan, combine water, wine, vinegar, Worcestershire Sauce, lemon juice, mustard, Tabasco, paprika, garlic, onion, 1 Tbsp (15 ml) vegetable oil, and 1/2 tsp (2 ml) salt. Bring to boil. Baste lamb with sauce, cooking 1 hour more, or to your liking. Meat is medium-rare when internal temperature reaches 150°F (65°C). Remove from grill and let stand 10-15 minutes before carving.

Blue Cheese Lamb Chops

SERVES 4

This simple yet elegant recipe is perfectly set off by fluffy mashed potatoes, maple buttered carrots, and Brussels sprouts with lemon wedges.

– R & W

8	rib or loin lamb chops	8
	vegetable oil	
	freshly ground black pepper	
1	garlic clove, chopped	1
1/2 cup	crumbled blue cheese	125 ml
2 Tbsp	whipping cream	30 ml

Using a small, sharp knife, trim and scrape the meat from the rib bones, about 2 inches (5 cm) from the tips, leaving just the meaty chop ends. Brush chops with oil and sprinkle with pepper, and press garlic into meat. Cover and let stand 2-3 hours.

In a small bowl, mix blue cheese and cream to form a paste. Set aside.

Preheat barbecue to medium.

Place chops on grill, and cook 5-6 minutes. Brush with oil, turn, and cook 5 minutes more. Remove from heat. Spread cheese top side of each chop, and return to grill until cheese melts.

Lamb with Cucumber Mint Sauce

Lamb is popular in many countries, and it's fun to "gussy it up" with flavours other than the traditional mint sauce. This recipe includes mint but has a distinctly Middle Eastern flavour.

– R & W

	pinch salt	
	coarsely ground black pepper	
2 Tbsp	olive oil	30 ml
8	1-inch (2.5-cm) loin lamb chops	8

For the Cucumber Mint Sauce:

	cucumber, peeled and chopped finely	1
1	mild onion, chopped finely	1
1	garlic clove, minced	1
1/4 cup	chopped fresh mint leaves	50 ml
1 cup	plain yogurt	250 ml
	dash of Tabasco Sauce	
	salt and freshly ground black pepper	

First, make the sauce. In a medium-sized bowl, combine all ingredients. Taste and adjust seasonings. Refrigerate for at least 1 hour before serving. Makes 2 cups.

Preheat barbecue to medium.

In a small bowl, mix salt, pepper, and olive oil. Brush lamb chops with oil, and place on oiled grill. Cook for 10-15 minutes, turning once and basting occasionally. Serve with Cucumber Mint Sauce.

Grilled Minted Lamb Chops

SERVES 4

8	1-inch (2.5-cm) loin lamb chops	8
	pinch salt	
	coarsely ground black pepper	
2 Tbsp	olive oil	30 ml

For the Mint Pesto:

1/2 cup	pine nuts, chopped finely	125 ml
1/2 cup	chopped fresh mint leaves	125 ml
1/3 cup	olive oil	75 ml
2 Tbsp	freshly grated parmesan cheese	30 ml
1/4 tsp	coarsely ground black pepper	1 ml
1 tsp	chopped garlic	5 ml

In a medium-sized bowl, mix together pesto ingredients and set aside.

Preheat barbecue to medium.

In a small bowl, mix salt, pepper, and olive oil. Brush lamb chops with oil, and place on oiled grill for 10-15 minutes, turning once and basting occasionally. Spoon 1 Tbsp (15 ml) of pesto on each lamb chop, and cook about 1 minute more. Serve hot with remaining pesto on the side.

We think the perfect way to cook lamb chops is on the barbecue. The smoke disappears, the fat doesn't collect in the bottom of your oven or broiler, and the chops acquire a lovely crispness. Turn the traditional mint into a pesto, and presto, gourmet lamb chops.

– R & W

Lamb in a Crock

It may sound like a crock, but I actually saw this dish cooked in small crockery pots when I was visiting the Middle East. Willa and I tried it using one of our old bean crocks and produced outstanding results. The lamb is not only incredibly flavourful, but it will fall from the bones, so don't splurge on an expensive cut.

– R

2 lb	lamb shanks, including bones	1 kg
	juice of 2 lemons	
	freshly ground black pepper	
1 tsp	salt	5 ml
1/2 tsp	finely chopped fresh oregano	2 ml
1/2 tsp	finely chopped fresh thyme	2 ml
1	bay leaf, chopped finely	1
2 Tbsp	olive oil	30 ml
	flour and water, for paste	

Preheat barbecue to medium-hot.

Cut shanks into serving-sized portions, and sprinkle with lemon juice, black pepper, salt, and herbs. Lay each portion on a piece of aluminum foil large enough to wrap it securely. Sprinkle olive oil on meat and wrap tightly in foil. Place packets in bean crock. Put on the lid, and seal it around the rim with a thick paste made from flour and water.

Place two bricks on the grill, just far enough apart to hold the base of the crock while leaving a space between the bricks for the heat to circulate. Close the barbecue lid, and cook for 2 1/2 hours. Remove crock from barbecue. Carefully chip away dried flour paste with a heavy blunt knife or a screwdriver. Lift crock lid and remove foil packets, opening them carefully to avoid the steam. Serve lamb with baked potatoes and Tomato and Bread Salad (page 219).

Spicy Skewered Lamb

SERVES 4

This is an excellent recipe to prepare ahead of time. If you're expecting guests for dinner on a busy day, marinate the lamb the day before. Serve with steamed rice and a Greek salad.

– R & W

1 cup	plain yogurt	250 ml
2 Tbsp	grated fresh ginger	30 ml
2 tsp	curry powder	10 ml
1/2 tsp	hot sauce	2 ml
1 tsp	salt	5 ml
2 lb	lean lamb meat, cut in cubes	1 kg
8	garlic cloves, sliced thinly	8

In a shallow glass dish, mix yogurt, ginger, curry, hot sauce, and salt. Add lamb, coating well, and then cover and refrigerate up to 24 hours. Stir occasionally.

Place 2 bricks on the grill and preheat to medium-hot. Soak 8-12 bamboo skewers in water.

Thread lamb cubes alternately with garlic slices onto bamboo skewers. Place across the bricks over the grill and cook 8 minutes, turning and basting with marinade frequently.

Plum Nutty Lamb

SERVES 4-6

It might be argued that this recipe is a combination of unrelated flavours. However, after trying it, we know you will want to repeat the experience. The recipe was developed at our summer house on the St. John River using the ingredients we had on hand — which happened to include Plum and Ginger Sauce.

– R & W

2	garlic cloves, chopped finely	2
2 Tbsp	canola oil	30 ml
1/4 cup	peanut butter	50 ml
2 Tbsp	white wine	30 ml
1 Tbsp	curry powder	15 ml
2 tsp	sugar	10 ml
2 lb	boneless lamb, cut in 2-inch (5-cm) cubes	1 kg
1	onion, quartered and separated into leaves	1
1/4 cup	peanuts, chopped finely	50 ml
1/2 cup	Plum and Ginger Sauce	125 ml

In a glass bowl, mix garlic, oil, peanut butter, white wine, curry powder and sugar. Add cubed lamb, and mix to coat thoroughly. Let stand 30 minutes.

Place two bricks on grill to hold skewers, and preheat barbecue to medium-hot.

Thread lamb cubes onto metal skewers, alternating them with pieces of onion. Roll skewers in chopped peanuts. Place skewers across bricks, and close barbecue lid. Cook 20-30 minutes, turning frequently. If meat browns too quickly, reduce heat. During last 5 minutes of cooking, baste lamb with Plum and Ginger Sauce (page 30). Serve hot, with extra sauce on the side.

Lamb in Pita

SERVES 6

1 1/2 lb	ground lamb	750 g
1/2 cup	finely chopped onion	125 ml
1 cup	chopped fresh parsley	250 ml
1 tsp	salt	5 ml
1/2 tsp	freshly ground black pepper	2 ml
1/4 tsp	mace	1 ml
1/2 tsp	paprika	2 ml
2 tsp	Worcestershire Sauce	10 ml
	vegetable oil	
6	pitas	6
2	tomatoes, chopped	2

These lamb "sausages" with our favourite Yogurt Dressing can be made in advance for a quick and easy lunch when guests arrive. Cooking them on skewers makes the job that much easier.

– R & W

For the Yogurt Dressing:

3/4 cup	plain yogurt	175 ml
1	small cucumber, seeded and grated	1
1	garlic clove, chopped	1
1 Tbsp	chopped fresh mint	15 ml
2 tsp	lemon juice	10 ml

Preheat barbecue to medium.

To prepare dressing, mix yogurt, cucumber, garlic, mint, and lemon juice in a small bowl. Serve immediately, or cover and refrigerate for up to 2 days.

In the large bowl of a food processor fitted with a steel blade, combine lamb, onion, parsley, salt, pepper, mace, paprika, and Worcestershire Sauce. Pulse until mixture forms a paste.

Divide the mixture into 12 portions. Form two 5 x 1 inch (12 x 2.5 cm) "sausages" on each skewer, wrapping the meat mixture around the skewer. Brush with oil, and cook on oiled grill 10-12 minutes, turning occasionally. They are ready when it there is no pink colour left. Remove sausages from skewers, and place in pitas with chopped tomatoes and Yogurt Dressing.

Lamb Fingers

SERVES 4

1 lb	ground lamb	500 g
1	egg, beaten	1
1 tsp	dried rosemary	5 ml
1/2 cup	fresh bread crumbs	125 ml
2 Tbsp	minced red pepper	30 ml
2 tsp	minced onion	10 ml
1 tsp	Worcestershire Sauce	5 ml
	dash of hot sauce	
1/4 tsp	freshly ground black pepper	1 ml

If you can't find ground lamb, don't hesitate to ask your butcher — a day or two in advance — to grind some for you. These burgers are shaped into fingers, perfect for pita pockets or rolls. They are also good served with rice or potatoes. Either way, have some Minted Yogurt Sauce (page 38) on hand.

– R & W

In a large bowl, mix lamb with all other ingredients. Shape into 16 fingers, and refrigerate 30 minutes.

Preheat barbecue to medium-hot.

Place lamb fingers on oiled rack, and cook 5 minutes on each side, until lightly browned. If they brown too quickly, reduce the heat or move the lamb fingers to a cooler part of the grill. Serve hot.

Lamb Loaf

This delicious recipe combines the flavour of lamb and the moistness of pork, producing a loaf that is equally delicious as a hot entrée or served cold sliced in sandwiches.

— R & W

1	small onion, diced	1
1	clove garlic, chopped finely	1
1 Tbsp	butter	15 ml
1 Tbsp	canola oil	15 ml
1/2	small red pepper, chopped	1/2
1 Tbsp	chopped fresh parsley	15 ml
1 tsp	dried thyme	5 ml
1 1/2 lb	ground lamb	750 g
1/4 lb	ground pork	125 g
1	egg, beaten lightly	1
1/4 cup	milk	50 ml
1 cup	bread crumbs	250 ml
1 tsp	salt	5 ml
	freshly ground black pepper	

Preheat barbecue to medium-hot.

In a skillet set over medium heat, sauté onion and garlic in butter and oil until onion is softened. In a large mixing bowl, combine onion mixture with remaining ingredients, mixing well. Form into a loaf, and place in a greased loaf pan covered with aluminum foil, or wrap tightly in foil. Place pan or foil packet on one side of barbecue, turning off element directly beneath it and leaving the other side of the grill on. Close barbecue lid, and cook 1 1/2 - 2 hours.

Lamb Burgers

Serve these with onion slices and Herb Mayonnaise (page 41) on crusty rolls. They'll put zing into your spring.

– R & W

1 lb	ground lamb	500 g
1	egg, beaten	1
1/2 tsp	freshly ground black pepper	2 ml
1 tsp	salt	5 ml
1	sprig fresh parsley, chopped	1
1/2 tsp	basil	2 ml
2	spring onions, chopped	2

Preheat grill to medium-hot.

In a bowl, mix together all ingredients, and form into 4 patties. Cook on oiled grill for 3-4 minutes on each side. Serve hot.

Pork

In the past decade, pork has undergone substantial changes in the manner in which it is raised. A leaner product, more acceptable to today's consumer, is the result of improved feeding techniques. Pork today has one-third fewer the calories it did some 10 years ago, and it's a healthy choice for the barbecue because much of the fat is lost during grilling. Most pork is cured for bacon or ham, but fresh pork comes in various cuts, and virtually all of them are quite suitable for barbecue cooking. Fresh pork is available year round but is more plentiful and lower in price in October and February. Like lamb, the paler pink the flesh, the younger the animal.

Pork roasts for rotisserie cooking should be boned and rolled to allow easier handling, cooking, and carving. Pork chops, a popular cut taken from the rib section, include part of the rib. Chops should be marbled. Trim most of the extra fat from around the edges, but be sure to leave a small amount to help baste and flavour the meat. Shoulder steaks are luscious and juicy, but they may be less tender than chops. Spare ribs for barbecuing should be partially precooked by boiling, braising, or pressure-cooking to assure that, after a quick grilling, they'll be thoroughly cooked, succulent, tender, and juicy. If you don't wish to precook ribs, we suggest cooking them on a rotisserie. Fresh pork sausage and cured hams also are perfect for grilling.

Pork requires less cooking today than in previous years, thanks to improved feeding and handling. It is necessary, though, to use normal precautions in preparing the raw product. Always wash hands, knives, and any utensils that come in contact with raw meat thoroughly. Pork should be cooked to an internal temperature of between 155°F (68°C) and 165°F (74°C) for safety and moistness. Cooking to a higher temperature will dry out most cuts of pork.

Spitted Pig Roast

SERVES 10-12

In Cuba, where we have enjoyed "puerco assado" (roast pork), all one needs is a safe and convenient place to lay a fire, a piece of corrugated iron to form a reflector, and a length of bamboo strong enough to hold the pig. The spit turns for six hours on manpower, as someone patiently turns it to keep the pig basting in its own juices. Allow about 12-15 minutes per pound (500 g) if roasting a stuffed pig outside in a sheltered but open barbecue. You can roast a "hollow" pig, if you want to save 2-3 minutes per pound. However, the stuffing itself is heavenly, and is well worth the longer cooking time.

— R & W

10-12 lb	pig, cleaned and ready for cooking	5-5.5 kg
	salt and freshly ground black pepper	
1/4 lb	melted butter	125 g
2	large onions, chopped	2
4	large apples, peel, cored, and chopped coarsely	4
1/4 cup	chopped fresh sage	50 ml
1/2	loaf bread, cubed	1/2
1 cup	apple juice	250 ml
	chopped fresh parsley	
	oil for greasing pig	
	melted butter for basting	

Spit-roasted pork is something everyone should experience at least once. I've roasted three suckling pigs over the years, although I've been amazed at how very difficult (if not impossible) it is to obtain a suckling pig, which should weigh in at around 8-10 pounds (3.75-5 kg). A young pig weighing 25-30 pounds (12.5-15 kg) dressed, can be cooked on a spit — if you have the proper equipment.

Preheat roasting pit by lighting charcoal or building a fire at least 1 hour prior to roasting. Wash pig's cavity with weak solution of baking soda and water. Rinse with fresh water, drain well, and pat dry. Sprinkle throughout with salt and pepper.

In a large roasting pan, melt butter, and sauté onion. Add chopped apple and sage, and stir well. Stir in bread cubes, apple juice, and parsley, mixing well. Season with salt and pepper. Fill cavity with stuffing, and stitch it closed, using twine and/or skewers, as you would close a turkey. Place a wooden peg or a corncob in pig's mouth to hold it open during roasting. Insert spit through pig, and use soft iron wire to attach pig to spit in several places. Bend both front and hind legs back, and secure them to spit. Bind a sheet of wire mesh over pig's abdomen to prevent the stuffing from falling out during cooking. Once secured, lightly grease exterior of pig, and set spit in place over coals. Position briquettes to leave a space for a metal drip pan to catch juices and fat. Add water to pan, replenishing as needed, to prevent it from drying out and catching fire.

As the pig turns slowly over the coals, keep the fire medium-hot, adding charcoal as needed. You may need 5-6 bags of charcoal, and it's better to have extra rather than run short. Baste occasionally with melted butter. When the pig is lightly browned, about halfway through the cooking process, scrape the glowing coals evenly to both ends of the pit. Leave the centre area clear, except for the drip pan, as the middle of the pig will be done long before the heavier ends. Continue roasting until a thermometer inserted in the haunch, clear of any bone, registers 160°F (70°C). Lift pig on spit and place on table or large tray. Remove spit and let pig rest for about 20 minutes before carving. Replace the wooden peg in the pig's mouth with a small apple. Remove metal mesh from pig's midsection, spoon out the stuffing, and serve it with pieces of pork and "crackling," the crisp, brown skin.

Herbed Pork Tenderloin

SERVES 6

Tender, herbed, lean, yet juicy sums up this great way to enjoy pork tenderloin. The herbs can be of your choosing, but they should be fresh rather than dried. Rosemary, thyme, oregano, and basil are all good partners for this dish.

– R & W

2	pork tenderloins 1 1/2 lb (750 g)	2
2	bunches fresh herbs	2
1/4 cup	canola or olive oil	50 ml
	freshly ground black pepper	

Preheat barbecue to hot.

Cut 4 12-inch (30-cm) lengths of heavy string and lay them vertically on work surface, evenly spaced along length of tenderloins. Lay half the herb sprigs across the string. Rub tenderloins with oil, season with pepper, and lay one on top of the herbs and string. Lay the other tenderloin on top, mismatching wide and narrow ends to create a uniform shape. Place the remaining herbs on top of the tenderloins, and secure bundle by tying strings tightly.

Brush bundle with oil, and place on hot grill. Reduce heat to medium, and cook, uncovered, for 45 minutes, turning frequently. Pork is ready when herbs are charred and internal temperature of pork is 155°F-160°F (65°C-70°C). Remove from heat, cut string, and remove and discard charred herbs. Let pork rest for 10 minutes before slicing on the diagonal.

Smoked Apple Pork Loin

My dad would never eat pork without a large serving of applesauce or apple jelly on the side, the perfect foil for the richness of pork. Here's a great recipe that combines the sweetness of apple and the duskiness of barbecue smoke to make pork loin heavenly fare.

– R

1 cup	apple juice	250 ml
1/4 cup	honey	50 ml
2 tsp	dry mustard	10 ml
1 tsp	ground cloves	5 ml
3 1/2 - 4 1/2 lb	centre-cut pork loin (backbone cut)	1.5 - 2 kg

In a small bowl, mix together apple juice, honey, mustard and cloves. Secure pork loin on rotisserie spit. Set aside.

Place drip pan or tray on grill, and add 1 cup (250 ml) water. Light the grill, and turn to medium. Close lid, and leave for 10 minutes. Add alder, hickory or apple wood chips to the hot rocks or tiles at one end of barbecue.

Put rotisserie in place. With lid closed, cook 20-25 minutes per pound (500 g), adding wood chips when smoke subsides. Replenish water in drip tray as necessary to keep fat and juices from burning. After pork has cooked 1 hour, baste every 20 minutes with glaze.

Pork is ready when internal temperature reaches 150°F-165°F (65°C-72°C).

Peanut Stuffed Pork

Pork and peanuts are a natural on the barbecue — watch your family clean up this dish.

– R & W

4	1-inch (2.5-cm) pork chops	4
1/4 cup	honey	50 ml
2 Tbsp	lemon juice	30 ml
1/3 cup	butter or margarine	75 ml
1 Tbsp	finely chopped onion	15 ml
1 Tbsp	finely chopped celery	15 ml
1 Tbsp	finely chopped parsley	15 ml
1/2 cup	bread crumbs	125 ml
1/4 cup	salted peanuts, chopped finely	50 ml
1/2 tsp	dried sage	2 ml
	freshly ground black pepper	

Using a sharp knife, make a pocket in each chop by cutting into the outer edge towards the bone. Set aside. Soak 8 toothpicks in water.

In a small dish, mix honey and lemon juice. Set aside.

Preheat barbecue to medium-hot.

In a frying pan set over medium heat, melt butter and sauté onion, celery and parsley. Stir in bread crumbs, peanuts, sage, and pepper. Stuff each pork chop, and seal edges by making an X with two toothpicks.

Place chops on oiled grill, cover, and cook 45-55 minutes or until meat is no longer pink. Brush frequently with honey and lemon sauce during the last 20 minutes.

Marinated Pork Chops

If you don't have time to marinate the pork, good results can be had by basting with the marinade during the last 5-10 minutes of cooking. Use nicely marbled chops for this recipe.

– R & W

6	1-2 inch (2.5-5 cm) pork chops, marbled	6
1	garlic clove, chopped	1
1/2 cup	apple cider	125 ml
2 Tbsp	lemon juice	30 ml
2 Tbsp	sugar	30 ml
2 tsp	Worcestershire Sauce	10 ml
1 cup	canola oil	250 ml
1 Tbsp	dry mustard	15 ml
	salt and freshly ground black pepper	

In a shallow glass dish, mix all ingredients except chops. Add chops, turning to coat, and refrigerate for 4 hours.

Preheat barbecue to medium.

Drain chops, reserve the marinade, and stir it well. Place chops on oiled grill, and cook 15-18 minutes, turning and basting frequently. Watch carefully to avoid scorching.

Far East Pork

We do enjoy pork with apples — applesauce, apple jelly, pickled apples, even apple stuffing. But when peaches are in season, I can't resist making Peach Chutney (page 33) and serving it with these fresh-flavoured chops.

– W

4	pork loin chops	4
1	large garlic clove, crushed	1
1/4 tsp	grated fresh ginger	1 ml
1/2 tsp	curry powder	2 ml
2 Tbsp	soy sauce	30 ml
1/4 cup	sherry	50 ml
1/4 cup	olive oil	50 ml
3 Tbsp	frozen orange juice concentrate, thawed	45 ml
1 tsp	freshly grated orange zest	5 ml

In a shallow glass dish, mix garlic, ginger, curry, soy sauce, sherry, olive oil, orange juice concentrate, and orange zest. Add chops, turning to coat both sides. Cover, and marinate 1-2 hours at room temperature.

Preheat barbecue to hot.

Drain chops, reserving marinade. Place chops on oiled grill, and cook 15-20 minutes, turning and basting occasionally with marinade. Serve with Peach Chutney.

Corn and Apple Stuffed Pork Pockets

SERVES 6

These colourful chops are almost a meal in themselves. Stuffed full of veggies and apple, they don't even need applesauce. To make the recipe easier, have your butcher cut the pockets in the pork chops.
— R & W

6	1-inch (2.5-cm) thick pork chops	6
1 cup	corn kernels	250 ml
3/4 cup	chopped red pepper	175 ml
3/4 cup	Granny Smith apple, cored and chopped	175 ml
1/2 cup	finely chopped red onion	125 ml
1/4 cup	chopped fresh cilantro	50 ml
2 Tbsp	apple vinegar	30 ml
2 Tbsp	vegetable oil	30 ml
1/4 tsp	salt	1 ml
1/4 tsp	freshly ground black pepper	1 ml

Preheat barbecue to medium.

Create a pocket in each pork chop by cutting in from outer edge towards the bone. Set aside.

In a medium-sized bowl, stir together remaining ingredients. Place 2 Tbsp (30 ml) in each pocket, and secure with skewers or toothpicks. Place chops on oiled grill, and cook 20-30 minutes, turning occasionally. Remove toothpicks before serving with any extra filling.

Citrus Pork

SERVES 4-6

You can use either pork chops or pork steaks for this recipe. Steaks will be luscious and juicy, but they can be tougher than chops.

– R & W

1 cup	orange juice	250 ml
1/4 cup	honey or corn syrup	50 ml
1/4 cup	canola oil	50 ml
1	garlic clove, crushed	1
1/2 tsp	curry powder	2 ml
1 tsp	salt	5 ml
6	pork steaks or chops	6

In a large, shallow glass dish, combine juice, honey, oil, garlic, curry and salt. Mix well. Add meat, and turn to coat. Cover and refrigerate for 1-2 hours, turning meat once.

Preheat barbecue to medium-hot.

Drain pork, reserving marinade. Place pork on oiled grill, and cook until browned underneath. Turn, baste with marinade, and continue cooking. Once the other side browns, turn and baste regularly for 15-20 minutes more. Pork should be cooked until it is no longer pink inside.

Marinades containing fruit juices have a tendency to burn, due to their sugar content. Keep a close eye on the grill, and turn meat frequently to avoid charring.

Maple Mustard Pork Steaks

SERVES 4

Dry mustard adds a nice tang to these grilled chops, while the maple syrup and vinegar create a sweet and sour complement. Simple and tasty.

– R & W

4	pork steaks	4
2 Tbsp	canola or olive oil	30 ml
1/4 cup	maple syrup	50 ml
1 Tbsp	dry mustard	15 ml
1 Tbsp	apple cider vinegar	15 ml

Preheat barbecue to medium-hot.

Trim steaks of excess fat, and slash edges to prevent curling. Brush with half the oil, and place on oiled grill. Close barbecue lid, and reduce heat.

Meanwhile, in a small bowl, mix remaining oil with maple syrup, mustard, and cider vinegar. Turn steaks when well browned, and brush cooked sides with sauce. Cook for 5-10 minutes more, then turn steaks and baste again. Meat should be juicy but not pink when done. Serve hot and sizzling.

Maple Ribs

SERVES 4-6

Beer and bay leaves flavour and tenderize these tasty ribs while they precook in a slow oven. The basting sauce is enriched with sweet and spicy ingredients. And don't throw the sauce away — reheat it, and put it on the table. Your guests will want to have extra to add to their potatoes and meat.

– R & W

3-4 lb	pork or beef ribs	1.5 - 2 kg
1	bottle beer	1
2	bay leaves	2
2	large onions, chopped	2
2	garlic cloves, chopped	2
2 Tbsp	canola oil	30 ml
1/2 cup	tomato ketchup or sauce	125 ml
1/4 cup	apple cider vinegar	50 ml
1 tsp	paprika	5 ml
1/2 tsp	dry mustard	2 ml
2 Tbsp	Worcestershire Sauce	30 ml
1 tsp	chili powder	5 ml
1/2 cup	maple syrup	125 ml
1/2 tsp	salt	2 ml
	freshly ground black pepper	
1 tsp	dried thyme flakes	5 ml

Preheat oven to 275°F (140°C).

Place ribs in large roaster with tightly fitting lid or cover, and pour beer over. Add bay leaves, onion, and garlic, and cover roaster. Bake for 3 hours. This slow cooking partially cooks the ribs and keeps them moist. Remove ribs from roaster, transfer to large bowl, and cover with plastic wrap to retain moisture.

Skim fat from roasting juices. Discard bay leaves, and transfer remaining liquid to small saucepan over medium heat. Add remaining ingredients, and stir well until sauce starts to boil. Remove from stove.

Preheat barbecue to medium.

Place ribs on oiled grill, and close the cover. Cook 2-3 minutes, watching for flare-ups. Open barbecue, and baste ribs with sauce. Turn and grill the other side. Baste again, and cook for a few more minutes, turning as required to prevent burning. Meat should separate easily from the bones. Serve hot.

Sweet-Hot Pineapple Ribs

SERVES 4

It's impossible to have too many barbecued rib recipes, and here is one more that should be in your Top Ten.

– R & W

4-6 lb	meaty pork loin back ribs	2-3 kg
1	bottle beer or ale	1
1	bay leaf	1
1 cup	crushed pineapple	250 ml
1/2 cup	brown sugar	125 ml
2 Tbsp	lemon juice	30 ml
2	garlic cloves, chopped	2
1/4 cup	grainy Dijon mustard	50 ml
1 tsp	paprika	5 ml
1/2 tsp	turmeric	2 ml
1 tsp	dry mustard	5 ml
1 tsp	salt	5 ml

Place ribs in large pot with beer or ale and bay leaf, and boil with lid on for 15-20 minutes. Remove from heat, and cool.

Meanwhile, in a heavy-based saucepan over medium heat, combine pineapple, brown sugar, lemon juice, garlic, and Dijon mustard. Cook, stirring frequently until bubbling. Set aside.

Preheat barbecue to medium.

Drain ribs, pat dry, and rub with mixture of paprika, turmeric, dry mustard, and salt. Lay ribs, bone-side down, on oiled grill. Close lid, and reduce heat to low.

Cook for 10 minutes, turning once. Continue cooking over low heat for 20-25 minutes more. If meat browns too quickly, even over low heat, turn off one side of grill and transfer ribs to that side. When ribs are nicely cooked and tender, baste with pineapple sauce, and cook 5-10 minutes more, until well glazed. Serve hot.

Spicy Dry Rub Ribs

SERVES 4

This dry-rub rib recipe is easier to cook than it is to say. It reminds me of the dry spareribs you can find in specialty Chinese restaurants. The smoky flavour generated from wood chips makes me think of the mysterious Far East.

– R

4-6 lb	meaty pork loin back ribs	2-3 kg
1/2 tsp	salt	2 ml
1/2 tsp	celery salt	2 ml
2 Tbsp	brown sugar	30 ml
1/2 tsp	dry mustard	2 ml
1 tsp	dried ginger	5 ml
1/2 tsp	turmeric	2 ml
1 tsp	garlic powder	5 ml
1/2 cup	tomato sauce	125 ml
2 Tbsp	soy sauce	30 ml
1/2 cup	brown sugar	125 ml

Preheat oven to 350º F (180º C).

In a small bowl, mix salt, celery salt, brown sugar, dry mustard, ginger, turmeric, and garlic powder. Rub well into ribs. Place in roasting pan, cover, and bake 1 hour.

In a small saucepan over medium heat, mix tomato sauce, soy sauce, and 1/2 cup (125 ml) brown sugar. Stirring frequently, heat until bubbling and well blended. Remove from heat, and let cool.

Preheat grill to medium.

Place ribs, bone-side down, on oiled grill. Reduce heat to low. Sprinkle 1 cup (250 ml) wood chips on hot rocks or briquettes, and close lid. Cook 20 minutes, turning ribs several times and watching for flare-ups. If ribs are browning too quickly, turn off one side of grill and transfer ribs to that side. Add more wood chips, if necessary. Grill 15-20 minutes more on low, and then baste with sauce. Turn frequently, and baste with sauce until ribs are tender and ready to eat.

If tapered rib ends cook too quickly or begin to burn, wrap them in aluminum foil.

Sweet and Sour Pork on Skewers

SERVES 4-6

The tang of malt vinegar and the sweetness of citrus and tomato work very well with the rich flavour of pork. Serve with fragrant hot rice.

– R & W

1 lb	boneless pork shoulder	500 g
1 Tbsp	light soy sauce	15 ml
1 Tbsp	canola oil	15 ml
8	cherry tomatoes	8
1	small green pepper, cut in chunks	1
12	pineapple chunks	12

For the Sweet and Sour Sauce:

1 cup	malt vinegar	250 ml
1 cup	white sugar	250 ml
4 tsp	salt	20 ml
1/2 cup	orange juice	125 ml
1/2 cup	pineapple juice	125 ml
1/2 cup	tomato paste	125 ml
1 Tbsp	cornstarch	15 ml

To make the sauce, combine everything but the cornstarch in a small saucepan over medium heat. Bring to a boil, and simmer for 10 minutes. Taste and add more salt, if necessary. Dissolve cornstarch in 1/2 cup (125 ml) of sauce, return to saucepan, and mix well. Cook 1-2 minutes more. Sauce should be almost the consistency and colour of ketchup. Remove from heat, and set aside.

Preheat barbecue to hot. Soak bamboo skewers in water for 30 minutes before using.

Cut pork into 1-inch (2.5-cm) chunks. In a glass bowl, mix soy sauce and oil, add pork, and toss to coat. Thread pork onto skewers alternately with pineapple, tomatoes, and green pepper. Place two bricks on grill, and lay skewers between them with ends of skewers resting on bricks.

Cook with lid closed for 15-20 minutes, turning frequently. Baste with sauce during last few minutes of cooking, watching for scorching. Serve hot.

Rotisserie Glazed Ham

SERVES 10-12

4-6 lb	precooked boned ham	2-3 kg
2 tsp	dry mustard	10 ml
18-20	whole cloves	18-20
	freshly ground black pepper	
1 cup	brown sugar	250 ml
2 Tbsp	table molasses	30 ml
1/2 cup	apple juice	125 ml

You've not tasted a truly delicious smoky ham until you've rotisserie-roasted one in the barbecue. The most difficult part of cooking ham in this fashion is getting it properly balanced on the spit.

– R & W

Preheat barbecue to medium-hot.

Place ham on spit, balancing it as evenly as possible. Secure well. Sprinkle ham with mustard, and rub well into meat. If ham is encased in fat, score in a diamond pattern, using a sharp knife. Push whole cloves into ham at regular intervals, leaving clove head protruding for easy removal later. Place spit in barbecue, and, with motor turning, check for clearance. Place drip pan under meat, and pour 1 cup (250 ml) water into pan. Turn heat to low, close lid, and cook for 45 minutes, until ham is sizzling and hot through. Add wood chips to smoker pan during last 30 minutes of cooking, if desired.

In a small bowl, combine sugar, molasses, and apple juice.

Open lid, baste ham with glaze, close lid, and cook 10-15 minutes more, until glaze is nicely browned. Be careful that glaze does not burn. Serve hot.

Cranberry Raisin Ham Slices

SERVES 4

When buying ham for the barbecue, ask your butcher for 5-6 ounce (150-175 g) slices, about 1 inch (2.5 cm) thick. Allow 1 slice per person.

– R & W

4	ham slices, with rinds	4
	whole cloves	
1/2 cup	brown sugar	125 ml
2 Tbsp	cornstarch	30 ml
1 1/2 cups	cranberry juice	375 ml
1/2 cup	orange juice	125 ml
1/2 cup	seedless raisins	125 ml
	oil, for basting	

Use a sharp knife to score edges of ham. Insert 2-3 cloves in the fat.

In a small saucepan, mix sugar and cornstarch, add juices, place over medium heat, and stir until mixture boils. Add raisins, and stir constantly until thickened.

Preheat barbecue to medium-hot.

Brush ham slices with oil, and place on oiled grill. Cook 15 minutes, turn, and brush well with glaze. Cook 10 minutes more, turn again, and brush the other side. Brush again just before serving. Serve ham with remaining sauce.

Mediterranean Sausages

SERVES 6 AS AN APPETIZER

This barbecue recipe is reminiscent of one of the hot hors d'oeuvres or meze *I enjoyed almost 20 years ago on the sunny island of Cyprus.*

– R

6	spicy pork sausages	6
18	sun-dried tomatoes	18
6	slices bacon	6
2 Tbsp	lemon juice	30 ml

Preheat grill to medium-hot. Soak 12 toothpicks in warm water.

In a small bowl, rehydrate sun-dried tomatoes in warm water for about 10 minutes.

Cut each sausage almost in half down its length. Place 3 tomatoes in slit of each sausage. Close sausages, and wrap each with a slice of bacon, securing with a toothpick at each end.

Place sausages on grill, and cook 20 minutes, turning regularly, until cooked through. During the last few minutes of cooking, baste sausage with lemon juice.

Lift from the grill, remove toothpicks, slice, and serve hot.

Sausage Skewers

You don't need to use expensive cuts of meat for the barbecue. Sausages or hot dogs can be turned into pretty tantalizing fare when grilled with Maritime Barbecue Sauce (page 29).

– R & W

1/2 cup	Maritime Barbecue Sauce	125 ml
2	small zucchini	2
2 lb	spiced sausage or large wieners	1 kg
1	large onion, quartered and separated into leaves	1
1	sweet yellow pepper, seeded and cut in large chunks	1

Preheat barbecue to medium-hot. Soak bamboo skewers for half an hour.

Cut zucchini and sausage or wieners into 1 1/2-inch (3.5-cm) pieces. Thread zucchini, sausage, onion, and pepper alternately on skewers. Leave 2 inches (5 cm) of skewer at each end for easy handling. Place two bricks on grill, and place skewers between them with ends resting on bricks.

Close barbecue lid and grill 12-15 minutes, turning frequently. Baste with Maritime Barbecue Sauce during last few minutes of cooking. Serve hot.

POULTRY: CHICKEN, DUCK & TURKEY

You need only to prowl the meat counter of your supermarket to see the wealth of poultry available today. Chicken, game hen, duck, turkey, and goose are commonplace these days. Sometimes you can also find quail, partridge and pheasant. More exotic birds, such as ostrich and emu are also making their debut in the ultra-lean categories. Add to this the variety of chicken — boneless, skinless, free-range, water-chilled, whole, quarters, halves, pieces and fillets both fresh and frozen — and the possibilities are endless. Some cuts, such as breast fillets, will cook quickly to perfection and remain moist and tender. Other portions, such as legs, thighs and wings, require longer, slower cooking for tenderness. Whole birds done on the rotisserie remain nicely moist as they baste in their own juices.

Poultry should be grilled in a covered barbecue, to produce moist, golden-brown meat with a tender skin. Grilled uncovered, poultry has a tendency to dry out, and the skin may burn. If your grill doesn't have a cover, simply tuck heavy-duty foil loosely over the food and grill. Poultry cooked directly on the grill must be constantly tended and turned to keep the skin from burning. Should you prefer to remove all skin and fat before grilling, you should brush the flesh lightly with oil so it doesn't stick to the grill.

The primary concern with poultry is to cook it sufficiently without overcooking it. Poultry must be cooked to an internal temperature of 185°F (90°C) before being eaten, to kill any possible bacteria. Partially precooking whole chicken or pieces in a microwave oven or pressure cooker or by parboiling ensures complete cooking in the barbecue without charring the exterior. The result is golden-brown, delicious fare, cooked completely through.

Tarragon Roasted Chicken

SERVES 6

1	large roasting chicken	1
2 tsp	salt	10 ml
2 tsp	freshly ground black pepper	10 ml
1/2 cup	fresh tarragon	125 ml
2	garlic cloves, chopped finely	2
1/4 cup	canola oil	50 ml
1 Tbsp	paprika	15 ml
2	medium-sized onions, coarsely chopped	2
2 cups	water, white wine, or chicken stock	500 ml
	salt and pepper to taste	

Using a roasting pan eliminates the possibility of flare-ups while still allowing for a unique, smoky barbecue flavour. Choose a large meaty chicken to feed a crowd.
– R & W

Preheat barbecue to medium-low.

Trim extra fat from chicken, then wash and pat dry with paper towel. In a small dish, combine garlic and oil, and rub over skin and inside of chicken. Sprinkle the cavity with salt and pepper, and place tarragon inside. Truss wings and legs to body. Sprinkle lightly with salt, pepper and paprika. Place a small rack into a large, oiled roasting pan. Add water, wine, or chicken stock along with chopped onion. Place chicken on rack and cover lightly with aluminum foil. Put roasting pan in barbecue, and close lid. Cook 15-20 minutes per pound (500 g), basting occasionally with pan juices. Chicken is ready when the leg can be moved easily.

Remove chicken from pan, reserving pan juices for gravy, and let rest for 10 minutes before carving. Taste for seasoning before serving.

Honey Ginger Chicken

SERVES 6

Rotisserie chicken is ideal for the barbecue because it requires so little attention. The cook can relax with the guests while the chicken bastes itself as it rotates. We prefer free-range chickens, as they are so moist and delicious.

– R & W

5-7 lb	whole chicken	2.5-3.5 kg
2 Tbsp	honey	30 ml
2 Tbsp	lemon juice	30 ml
1 Tbsp	grated fresh ginger	15 ml
1/2 tsp	salt	2 ml
1/4 tsp	cayenne pepper	1 ml
1/2 cup	vegetable oil or citrus flavoured oil	125 ml

Preheat barbecue to medium-hot.

Trim extra fat from chicken, truss it, and mount it on the rotisserie. Put drip pan in place, and add water. Turn barbecue to low. When chicken is turning properly, close barbecue lid.

In a glass bowl, mix honey, lemon juice, ginger, salt, and pepper. Gradually incorporate the oil, mixing well. After 30 minutes, baste chicken lightly with glaze. Baste at regular intervals, adding water to drip pan as required.

Chicken should be beautifully brown and done in 2-3 hours, when its internal temperature reaches 180°F (85°C) and the legs wiggle easily when pulled.

Thai Chicken

SERVES 4-6

Now that many "exotic" spices and herbs are available at most markets, recipes like this are becoming easy adventures into world cuisine. The first bottle of Thai fish sauce I bought leaked its contents into my luggage during an international flight. Although the whiff of fish sauce still takes me back to this mishap, the exquisite flavour it brings to a dish like Thai Chicken is well worth the painful memories. Serve this with rice and fresh tomato salad.

– R

3-4 lb	frying chicken	2 kg
1 Tbsp	lemon zest	15 ml
1/2 cup	chicken broth	125 ml
2 Tbsp	Thai fish sauce	30 ml
2 Tbsp	lime juice	30 ml
1/4 cup	canola oil	50 ml
2 Tbsp	sugar	30 ml
1 Tbsp	soy sauce	15 ml
3	garlic cloves, chopped finely	3
1 Tbsp	dried mint flakes	15 ml
2 tsp	chili powder	10 ml
1/2 tsp	cayenne pepper	2 ml
1/4 cup	fresh chopped basil	50 ml
	fresh chopped cilantro, to garnish	

Cut chicken into two halves through breast and back bones. In a small glass bowl, mix remaining ingredients. Place chicken in heavy plastic bag, and pour in marinade. Seal bag, and refrigerate for 1-2 hours, turning once or twice. Remove chicken from marinade, and place in shallow glass baking dish. Cover with plastic wrap, and vent at one end. Microwave at high setting for 8-9 minutes, turning once during cooking.

Preheat barbecue to medium-hot.

Place chicken halves on lightly oiled grill. Close barbecue lid and cook 10-12 minutes. Turn and baste chicken, and cook 10-12 minutes more. Turn once again, and check that chicken is nicely browned and cooked through. Juices should run clear when thickest piece is pierced through with a fork or skewer. Garnish with cilantro and serve hot.

Teriyaki Chicken Salad

SERVES 4 AS A SIDE DISH

3	chicken pieces (breast, thigh, and leg)	3
2 Tbsp	canola oil	30 ml
1 tsp	sesame oil	5 ml
1 Tbsp	soy sauce	15 ml
1 Tbsp	molasses	15 ml
1 lb	large mushrooms, halved	500 g
3	bok choy (Chinese cabbage) stalks	3
3	green onions	3

For the Teriyaki Dressing:

1 Tbsp	grated fresh ginger	15 ml
2	garlic cloves, minced	2
1/4 cup	chopped fresh cilantro or parsley	50 ml
2 Tbsp	rice wine vinegar	30 ml
3 Tbsp	soy sauce	45 ml
1/4 cup	canola oil	50 ml
1 Tbsp	sesame oil	15 ml
	salt and freshly ground black pepper	
	toasted sesame seeds	

Grilling chicken pieces marinated in teriyaki turns a traditional chicken salad into an Oriental delight. Use both white and dark meat to develop the unique flavour in this salad.
– R & W

Preheat barbecue to medium-hot.

Partially cook chicken in microwave for 6 minutes at high setting. Remove and set aside.

Meanwhile, in a small bowl, mix canola and sesame oils, soy sauce, and molasses. Lightly brush on chicken pieces, reserving excess.

Place chicken on oiled grill, and cook about 12 minutes, turning once and basting. Juices should run clear when chicken is pierced at thickest point. Transfer chicken to cutting board. When cool enough to handle, remove meat from bones, and chop into bite-sized pieces. Cover and set aside to keep warm.

In a small bowl, blend together dressing ingredients, reserving toasted sesame seeds for garnish.

Increase barbecue heat. Lightly brush mushrooms, green onions, and bok choy with remaining glaze. Quickly sear on very hot grill, and chop bok choy and green onions into bite-sized pieces. Toss chicken and vegetables with dressing, and pile on plates, sprinkling with toasted sesame seeds.

Spicy Citrus Chicken

SERVES 4

Cinnamon and nutmeg will spice up a package of chicken pieces and prove a hit at your next potluck barbecue. This recipe is inexpensive, exotic, and quick. Quantities can easily be doubled for larger gatherings.

– R & W

3 lb	chicken, cut in 8 pieces	1.5 kg
1 tsp	paprika	5 ml
1/2 tsp	cinnamon	2 ml
1/2 tsp	nutmeg	2 ml
1/4 tsp	salt	1 ml
	freshly ground black pepper	
1/2 cup	melted butter	125 ml
6 oz	frozen orange juice concentrate, thawed	175 ml

Preheat barbecue to medium.

Remove excess fat from chicken pieces. Place on oiled grill over drip pan. Cook, turning occasionally, 45-60 minutes, or until tender.

Meanwhile, in a large saucepan over medium-low heat, combine remaining ingredients. Cook for 3-4 minutes, stirring occasionally, until heated. Baste chicken pieces with sauce during last 15 minutes of cooking. Serve with rice or potatoes and remaining warm basting sauce.

Sun-Dried Tomato Chili Chicken

SERVES 4

We barbecue chicken more often than any other meat, and we're constantly on the lookout for new recipes, often "borrowing" marinades and sauces from pork, seafood, or beef recipes. Don't hesitate to take our recipes and substitute them on your favourite meat. (Maybe that's where they were in the first place.)
– R & W

8	chicken pieces (breasts and thighs)	8
3 Tbsp	butter, softened	45 ml
2 Tbsp	sun-dried tomato paste	30 ml
1	lime, freshly squeezed juice and zest	1
2 tsp	chili sauce	10 ml
	oil, for basting	
	lime wedges to garnish	

Using your fingertips, gently lift the skin from the chicken breasts and thighs.

In a small bowl, mix butter, sun-dried tomato paste, lime zest, and chili sauce. Spread half of mixture evenly under skin of the chicken pieces. Mix remaining paste with lime juice, and reserve for basting.

Preheat barbecue to medium-hot.

Place oiled chicken on oiled grill. Cook 20-30 minutes, turning and basting occasionally with oil. Brush with reserved paste during last 10 minutes, turning frequently. Juices should run clear when thickest piece is pierced through with a fork or skewer. Arrange chicken on large platter, and garnish with lime wedges.

Chicken Paprikash

*Chicken Paprikash on the barbecue? Yes — it's one of my favourites.
Try to buy sweet Hungarian paprika, available in mild, half-sweet,
or hot. Spanish paprika is always mild and is often used more for
colour than flavour. You can use it if you can't find Hungarian
paprika.*

— W

3 Tbsp	lemon juice	45 ml
3 Tbsp	melted butter	45 ml
1	garlic clove, minced	1
1 tsp	salt	5 ml
1 tsp	sweet Hungarian paprika	5 ml
	freshly ground black pepper	
3 lb	chicken, cut into serving pieces	1.5 kg
	oil or melted butter, for basting	

For the Paprika Sauce:

3 Tbsp	butter	45 ml
2 Tbsp	diced onion	30 ml
1/2 cup	chopped mushrooms	125 ml
1 Tbsp	flour	15 ml
2 tsp	paprika	10 ml
1 cup	chicken broth	250 ml

1/2 cup	tomato sauce	125 ml
2 Tbsp	dry sherry	30 ml
1/2 cup	sour cream	125 ml
	chopped fresh parsley, to garnish	

In a shallow glass dish, combine lemon juice, butter, garlic, salt, paprika, and pepper. Place chicken in dish, and turn to coat well. Cover and refrigerate for at least 8 hours, or overnight.

Preheat barbecue to medium.

Drain chicken, and discard marinade. Place chicken on oiled grill, and cook for 15 minutes. Turn frequently, and cook 15-25 minutes longer, basting occasionally with oil or melted butter, until juices run clear when chicken is pierced with a fork or skewer.

Meanwhile, prepare sauce by melting butter in a medium-sized saucepan. Sauté onion for 5 minutes. Add mushrooms and sauté until tender. Add flour, and bring to a boil, stirring constantly. Remove from heat, and stir in paprika. Return to medium heat, and stir in chicken broth and tomato sauce. Cook, stirring constantly, until sauce thickens. Stir in sherry. Remove from heat, and stir in sour cream. Spoon sauce over chicken pieces, and sprinkle with chopped parsley.

Fruited Chicken and Shrimp Kebabs

SERVES 6

6	skinless, boneless chicken breasts	6
12	large shelled shrimp, with tails	12
2	oranges, cut in 6 wedges	2
	salt and freshly ground black pepper	
1 cup	apricot preserves	250 ml
1/3 cup	rhubarb chutney	75 ml
1 Tbsp	soy sauce	15 ml
1 Tbsp	wine vinegar	15 ml

Ross once asked me whether I wanted chicken or shrimp. I simply answered "Yes." This is what I got. You can easily substitute peach preserves and tomato chutney.

– W

Preheat barbecue to medium-hot.

Cut each chicken breast into 4 pieces. Thread chicken onto oiled metal skewers, alternating with shrimp and orange wedges. Sprinkle with salt and pepper.

In a small bowl, mix remaining ingredients.

Place skewers on rack, and grill 5 minutes. Brush with fruit sauce, turn, and cook 5 minutes more. Brush again with sauce, turn, and cook 2 minutes more. Serve with remaining sauce as a dip.

Tandoori Chicken

SERVES 2-4

We've found that a closed barbecue can produce dishes as tasty as those cooked in a traditional Indian tandoor oven built of bricks and clay. This "tandoor" dish needs to be marinated for several hours to develop its unique flavour. Serve with basmati rice and cucumber salad.

— R & W

2 Tbsp	lemon juice	30 ml
1 cup	plain yogurt	250 ml
4	garlic cloves, chopped finely	4
1 Tbsp	grated fresh ginger	15 ml
1 tsp	allspice	5 ml
2 tsp	cumin	10 ml
1 tsp	coriander or cardamom	5 ml
1/2 tsp	cayenne pepper	2 ml
1/2 tsp	turmeric	2 ml
4	skinless, boneless chicken breasts	4

In a glass baking dish, combine everything except chicken. Mix well before adding chicken breasts. Coat well on all sides, and marinate at least 1 hour, turning occasionally.

Preheat barbecue to medium-hot.

Place chicken on oiled grill, and cook 8-10 minutes, turning at least once. Serve hot.

Pear Stuffed Chicken Breasts

SERVES 4

1/2 cup	honey	125 ml
2 Tbsp	vegetable oil	30 ml
2 tsp	dry mustard	10 ml
	freshly squeezed juice and zest of 1 lemon	
4	skinless, boneless chicken breasts	4
2 Tbsp	sugar	30 ml
1/4 tsp	cinnamon	1 ml
2	pears, peeled and sliced thinly	2

Preheat barbecue to medium.

In a small bowl, mix honey, vegetable oil, mustard, lemon juice, and zest. Cover and set aside.

Place chicken breasts between two pieces of waxed paper. Pound gently to 1/8-inch (3-mm) thickness. In a small bowl, mix sugar and cinnamon, and toss pear slices to coat. Divide pear slices among flattened chicken breasts, wrap meat around filling, and secure with toothpicks.

Cook chicken on oiled grill in covered barbecue 20-25 minutes, turning after 10 minutes, and basting with mustard glaze. Turn and baste both sides. Remove toothpicks, and serve with extra sauce on the side.

When we lived in Toronto, we had a pear tree in our little backyard. Every other year we had more pears than we could use. We gave them to everyone, and then developed recipes to use the rest. This is a perennial favourite.

– R & W

Chicken in the Bag

If you're fortunate enough to bag some chicken breasts, try this unique barbecue method for succulent, moist, and delicious results. You'll need a brown paper bag and a wooden clothespin.

— R & W

4	boneless chicken breasts	4
2 Tbsp	chopped fresh parsley	30 ml
1/4 cup	Italian dressing or barbecue sauce	50 ml
2 Tbsp	canola oil	30 ml
	salt and freshly ground black pepper	

Preheat barbecue to medium-hot.

Place two bricks on grill, and set a wire cooking rack on top.

Brush chicken breasts with Italian dressing or barbecue sauce and sprinkle with parsley, salt, and pepper. Rub oil on inside surface of paper bag and place chicken inside bag. Fold closed, and secure with clothespin. Lay bag on rack, close lid, and cook 15-20 minutes. The bag will puff up during cooking and should be removed from the grill carefully, as it contains scalding steam. Pierce bag with fork to let steam escape, and open with caution.

Chicken Pita

Pitas make a nice change from sliced bread. Willa always looks forward to these pockets for lunch, as they contain several of her favourite things — chicken, lime, and avocado.

– R

1/2 cup	lime juice	125 ml
1/2 tsp	chopped fresh garlic	2 ml
1/2 tsp	cumin	2 ml
1/4 tsp	chopped fresh rosemary	1 ml
4	boneless, skinless chicken breasts, halved	4

For the Guacamole:

2	medium-sized avocados, stoned and peeled	2
1/4 tsp	hot sauce	1 ml
1/2 tsp	salt	2 ml
1/2 cup	finely chopped ripe tomato	125 ml
1/4 cup	thinly sliced green onions	50 ml
2 Tbsp	chopped fresh cilantro or parsley	30 ml

1	lime, cut in wedges	1
4	6-inch (15-cm) pitas	4

Guacamole makes a great appetizer served with tortilla chipes.

In a shallow glass dish, combine 1/3 cup (75 ml) lime juice, garlic, cumin, and rosemary. Add chicken, and turn to coat. Cover with plastic wrap, and refrigerate for at least 30 minutes.

In medium-sized bowl or food processor, make guacamole by blending avocados with hot sauce, salt, and lime juice. Stir in tomatoes, onions, and cilantro. Season with extra hot sauce, if necessary.

Preheat barbecue to medium.

Remove chicken from marinade, and drain, reserving marinade. Place chicken on oiled grill. Cook 12-15 minutes, turning and basting occasionally, until chicken is tender and juices run clear. Remove chicken from grill. Cut pitas in half and warm on grill for 2-4 minutes. Divide guacamole among pita pockets, and place one chicken breast in each. Serve with lime wedges and extra guacamole.

Chicken Spinach Bundles

SERVES 4

1 cup	ricotta cheese	250 ml
10 oz	spinach, blanched and chopped	300 g
1/2 tsp	salt	2 ml
1 tsp	coarsely ground black pepper	5 ml
1 Tbsp	chopped fresh basil	15 ml
4	chicken breasts	4
	vegetable oil	

Preheat barbecue to medium.

In a medium-sized bowl, combine ricotta cheese, spinach, salt, pepper, and basil. Gently loosen skin from chicken breasts, and stuff with ricotta mixture. Secure with toothpicks, and brush with oil. Place on oiled grill over drip pan and grill, turning occasionally, 25-35 minutes, until chicken is tender and juices run clear. Remove toothpicks before serving.

The skin is left on these chicken breasts, giving a wonderfully crispy outer shell. Sometimes we use whole legs, for those who prefer dark meat.
– R & W

Hot Lemonade Chicken Wings

These wings are great served hot off the grill, but they also make a nice addition to any picnic. Make a jug of ice-cold lemonade to take along.

– R & W

3 lb	chicken wings	1.5 kg
6 oz	frozen lemonade concentrate, thawed	175 ml
3 Tbsp	Worcestershire Sauce	45 ml
1/4 tsp	hot sauce (Tabasco, or your favourite)	1 ml
1/2 tsp	dried oregano	2 ml
1/2 tsp	dried thyme	2 ml
1/2 tsp	chopped fresh garlic	2 ml
1/2 tsp	salt	2 ml
1/2 tsp	freshly ground black pepper	2 ml

Cut chicken wings into 3 pieces, using the meatier sections and saving the tips for stock.

In a shallow glass dish, stir together the remaining ingredients. Add chicken. Refrigerate for at least 8 hours or overnight, turning occasionally.

Preheat barbecue to medium.

Place chicken pieces on oiled grill. Cook 20-25 minutes, basting and turning frequently, until chicken is tender.

Honey Mustard Chicken Wings

SERVES 8

3 lb	chicken wings	1.5 kg
1/2 cup	honey mustard	125 ml
1/2 cup	vegetable oil	125 ml
1/4 cup	lemon juice	50 ml
1/4 cup	soy sauce	50 ml
1/4 cup	sesame seeds	50 ml
2 tsp	chili flakes	10 ml
3	garlic cloves, minced	3
1 tsp	freshly ground black pepper	5 ml

Sweet and sticky, finger-lickin' good, these wings are guaranteed to bring everyone back looking for seconds. Serve them at informal get-togethers as an appetizer or as part of a buffet. They are good with carrot and celery sticks and your favourite blue cheese dressing.
– R & W

Using a sharp knife or kitchen shears, cut wings in 3 pieces, using the meatier sections and reserving tips for chicken stock.

In a shallow glass dish, whisk mustard and oil until smooth. Slowly whisk in lemon juice and soy sauce. Add sesame seeds, chili flakes, garlic, and pepper, and mix well. Add chicken, cover, and refrigerate overnight.

Preheat barbecue to medium.

Remove chicken from marinade, and place on oiled grill. Cook 20-25 minutes, basting occasionally, until wings are tender and browned.

Chicken Liver Kebabs

Although this recipe starts on top of the stove, its real flavour develops on the grill. Serve with potatoes, rice, or pasta and Zucchini Roast (page 211).
– R & W

2 Tbsp	vegetable oil	30 ml
1	onion, chopped finely	1
1	clove garlic, chopped finely	1
1/4 cup	sherry	50 ml
1/2 tsp	hot sauce	2 ml
1 1/2 tsp	molasses	7 ml
1 tsp	freshly ground black pepper	5 ml
	salt	
1 lb	chicken livers, cleaned and trimmed	500 g
20	water chestnuts	20
1	sweet red or yellow pepper, cut in bite-sized pieces	1

In a small saucepan, heat oil, and sauté onion until soft. Add garlic, sherry, hot sauce, molasses and pepper. Season with salt to taste. Bring to a boil, reduce heat, and add chicken livers. Simmer for 1 minute to firm the liver. Remove from heat, and refrigerate for 2 hours, to allow the flavours to develop.

Preheat barbecue to medium, and soak bamboo skewers in water.

Remove livers from marinade, draining slightly, and thread onto skewers, alternating them with water chestnuts and pepper pieces.

Place on oiled grill, and cook for 6-8 minutes, turning and basting occasionally with reserved marinade.

Caesar Chicken Burgers

SERVES 4-6

Willa and I devised this burger after enjoying a Caesar salad with grilled chicken breast. You can substitute beef if you like, but ground chicken or turkey is best in this unique burger. It is particularly important to cook these thoroughly. If you like Caesar salad, you'll love these burgers.

– R

1	egg, lightly beaten	1
1 1/2 lb	ground chicken or turkey	750 g
1/4 cup	grated parmesan cheese	50 ml
1/3 cup	dry bread crumbs	75 ml
3 Tbsp	milk	45 ml
2 Tbsp	anchovy paste	30 ml
1 Tbsp	Worcestershire Sauce	15 ml
	zest of 1 lemon	
1 tsp	salt	5 ml
1 tsp	freshly ground black pepper	5 ml
1	garlic clove, chopped finely	1
2 Tbsp	canola oil	30 ml
6	Italian-style crusty rolls	6
	romaine lettuce, mayonnaise, and parmesan cheese, to serve	

Preheat barbecue to medium.

In a large mixing bowl, combine beaten egg, ground meat, parmesan cheese, bread crumbs, milk, anchovy paste, and Worcestershire Sauce. Mix well. Add lemon zest, salt, and pepper, and mix again. Form into 6 patties.

Place patties on oiled grill, and cook 5 minutes. Turn and cook 5-7 minutes more, until all traces of pink are gone.

In a small bowl, mix canola oil with garlic, and brush onto cut rolls. Grill until lightly toasted. Put burgers together with lettuce, mayonnaise, and a sprinkling of parmesan cheese.

Glazed Duck Breasts

SERVES 4

2	duck breasts, with skin	2
1	garlic clove, minced	1
1/2 cup	apricot jam	125 ml
3 Tbsp	Dijon mustard	45 ml
3 Tbsp	soy sauce	45 ml
3 Tbsp	honey	45 ml
	salt	
	freshly ground black pepper	

Preheat barbecue to medium.

In a small saucepan, mix garlic, apricot jam, mustard, soy sauce, and honey. Bring to a boil and simmer for several minutes. Set aside to cool.

Using a sharp knife, score breast skin with an X to allow excess fat to drain. Season lightly with salt and pepper, and place breasts on grill, skin-side down. Cook 6 minutes. Baste with apricot glaze and turn. Cook 5-6 minutes more, being careful they don't burn (turn down heat or move duck to cooler part of grill if necessary). Baste again, turn, and cook for 1-2 minutes more, until browned and crisp. Remove from heat. Slice breasts on the bias, and serve with remaining apricot glaze.

Duck breasts can be difficult to find. If you have a good butcher, ask him to remove the breasts for you, and take home the rest of the bird for stock or to freeze and cook later. A duck is much like a chicken, so don't hesitate to buy whole ducks and prepare them yourself.
– R & W

Marma-Duck

We enjoy duck and often roast one at Christmas. Because duck is very fat, cooking it on the barbecue works well. Marmalade and the barbecue spit make this version of duck à l'orange simple as well as elegant.

– W

5 lb	duck	2.5 kg
1 tsp	salt	5 ml
1	garlic clove, crushed	1
	freshly ground black pepper	
2	oranges, quartered	2
1/2 cup	orange marmalade	125 ml

Wash duck under cold water, drain well, and pat dry. Fasten neck skin over back, using small metal skewers or toothpicks. Season cavity with salt and pepper, and insert orange quarters. Secure opening with safety pins or sew shut with twine. Insert spit through centre of duck, making sure it is balanced.

Preheat barbecue to medium.

Cook duck on spit over barbecue for about 2 hours, pricking the skin with a fork occasionally to drain excess fat. When duck is cooked through, spread marmalade all over, and cook 10 minutes more to glaze. Remove from spit, and let stand 10 minutes before serving.

Teriyaki Cornish Hen

SERVES 4

Rock Cornish game hens usually weigh about 1 1/4 pounds (625 g), just big enough for a nice dinner for two. Like any poultry, they cook well on the barbecue, either whole on the spit or flattened on the grill. Any chicken recipe works well using these delicately flavoured all-white-meat birds.

– R & W

2	Rock Cornish game hens	2
	sesame oil	
	salt	
	freshly ground black pepper	
1/2 cup	soy sauce	125 ml
1/4 cup	white wine	50 ml
1/4 cup	rice vinegar	50 ml
1/3 cup	sugar	75 ml
1	garlic clove, crushed	1
1 inch	fresh ginger, crushed	2.5 cm
	peel from 1/4 lemon	

Preheat barbecue to medium-low.

Wash game hens in cold water, drain well, and pat dry. Split birds down centre of backbone. Open and flatten by pressing on the breast with the heel of your hand. To ensure the bird remains flat and open during cooking, insert two skewers horizontally through each hen. This also allows for easy handling. Brush with sesame oil, and sprinkle with salt and pepper.

Place birds skin-side down on oiled grill. Cook about 45 minutes, turning several times. The birds are done when meat near the bone is no longer pink and juices run clear.

Meanwhile, in a small saucepan, combine soy sauce, wine, vinegar, sugar, garlic, ginger, and lemon peel. Bring to a boil, reduce heat, and simmer until sauce is reduced by about half and begins to thicken. Remove garlic, ginger, and lemon peel.

During last 10 minutes of cooking, baste birds frequently with sauce. Take birds from grill, remove skewers, and cut in half. Serve with steamed rice and extra teriyaki sauce on the side.

Far East Quail

If you have access to an Oriental market, purchase some five-spice powder. If you don't, simply mix your own using the spices we have substituted, which are all quite readily available. If quail is unavailable, substitute a Cornish game hen, cut in half.

— R & W

4	quail, cleaned	4
2 tsp	cinnamon	10 ml
2 tsp	cumin	10 ml
2 tsp	freshly ground black pepper	10 ml
1/8 tsp	ground cloves	2.5 ml
1	small onion, chopped finely	1
1	garlic clove, chopped finely	1
4 Tbsp	honey	60 ml
2 Tbsp	soy sauce	30 ml

To serve:

1/2	head lettuce	1/2
2	sliced spring onions	2
	thinly sliced peel of 1 orange	

Using a pair of heavy-duty kitchen shears, cut along the backbones of the quail, removing bones. Flatten each bird, using the heel of your hand. Secure the quail by inserting two skewers in an X through each bird. Set aside.

In a small bowl, mix cinnamon, cumin, pepper, cloves, onion, garlic, honey, and soy sauce. Blend thoroughly.

Place quail in a large baking dish, and pour marinade over them. Turn to coat, and cover with plastic wrap. Refrigerate for 8 hours, or overnight.

Preheat barbecue to medium.

Remove quail from marinade, drain, and cook on oiled grill 15-20 minutes, basting occasionally with marinade, and turning once. Remove when golden brown.

To serve, thinly slice lettuce, and arrange on a large serving platter. Place quail on top, and sprinkle with spring onions and orange peel.

Grilled Turkey

SERVES 6-8 (WITH LEFTOVERS)

Use fresh rather than frozen turkey when grilling, as fresh meat will not dry out as quickly. Have your butcher cut a small fresh turkey in half for this recipe. The turkey needs to cook slowly to develop full flavour. For an even bigger flavour, baste with Moshe's Marinating Oil (page 26).

– R & W

8-10 lb	turkey, cut in half	4-5 kg
	canola oil *or* Moshe's Marinating Oil	
	paprika	
2 cups	fresh or frozen cranberries	500 ml
1	small apple, peeled and cored	1
1	small onion, diced	1
1 cup	brown sugar	250 ml
1/2 cup	tomato ketchup	125 ml
2 Tbsp	cider vinegar	30 ml
1 Tbsp	grated fresh ginger	15 ml
1 tsp	salt	5 ml
1 tsp	freshly ground black pepper	5 ml
1 Tbsp	orange zest	15 ml

Brush turkey with oil, and sprinkle with paprika. One at a time, microwave turkey halves, cut-side down, 10 minutes on high setting.

Preheat barbecue to medium-hot.

Place turkey halves, cut-side down, on oiled grill. Reduce heat to low and cook 45 minutes, basting once with oil. Watch for flare-ups. Turn turkey once after basting, and cook for 10 minutes only, then turn skin-side up again. If turkey browns too quickly, move to cooler position on barbecue, and lower heat. Continue to cook at low heat for another 30-45 minutes, until turkey leg wiggles easily when pulled and thermometer in breast indicates at least 165°F (75°C).

Meanwhile, combine cranberries with remaining ingredients in a small saucepan, and simmer over medium heat, until sauce is boiling and thickened. Set aside. Baste turkey once again during last few minutes of cooking. Remove from grill, and let stand 10 minutes before carving.

Maple Smoked Rotisserie Turkey

SERVES 6-8 (WITH LEFTOVERS)

This recipe needs two days to complete, but the results are quite spectacular. As with other turkey recipes, the secret lies in not over-cooking, and a fresh bird will be moister than a frozen one. Brining a turkey produces a moist and succulent bird, whether it's fresh or frozen. The unique maple-smoked flavour makes this turkey a holiday favourite.

– R & W

9-10 lb	fresh turkey, cleaned	4.5-5 kg
1/2 cup	coarse salt	125 ml
1/4 cup	maple syrup	50 ml
1/4 cup	brown sugar	50 ml
4 cups	apple juice	1 litre
1 Tbsp	freshly ground black pepper	15 ml
1	bay leaf, crushed	1
2	sprigs fresh thyme	2
	maple syrup, for basting	

In a plastic or glass container large enough to hold both turkey and brine solution, mix salt, syrup, sugar and apple juice with seasonings. Stir well, until salt and sugar are completely dissolved. Rinse turkey, removing excess fat. Immerse completely in brine, and keep overnight in a cool place. The following day, remove turkey from brine, and let air-dry for about 1 1/2 hours in a cool place.

Preheat barbecue to medium.

Balance turkey on rotisserie, allowing cavity to remain partially open to allow smoke to circulate inside. Place drip pan under turkey, and add 1 cup (250 ml) water to the pan. In a small metal tray or pan (disposable aluminum pans work well), place about 3 cups (750 ml) of wet alder or maple chips. Set pan over hottest portion of grill, so that smoke occurs after about 30 minutes. You may have to adjust heat and pan until this works as you want it. Check occasionally to be sure rotisserie is working properly and smoke is generating nicely. Cook 2 1/2 hours, until the turkey reaches an internal temperature of 185°F (85°C). Baste turkey with extra maple syrup during last 30 minutes of cooking.

Herb Turkey Breast in Foil

SERVES 6

3-5 lb	turkey breast half, with skin	1.5-2.5 kg
1/2 cup	diced onion	125 ml
1/4 cup	diced celery	50 ml
1/4 cup	finely diced carrot	50 ml
2	sprigs fresh sage	2
1 tsp	dried thyme	5 ml
	zest of 1 lemon	
1/4 cup	white wine	50 ml
	salt and freshly ground black pepper	

This low-fat recipe uses fresh herbs to enhance the delicate flavour of turkey breast. Foil cookery retains a tender moistness that is not always easy to achieve through grilling. Serve the sliced turkey breast as is, or use it to make delicious sandwiches.

– R & W

Place turkey breast in microwave-safe baking dish. In a small bowl, mix vegetables with herbs and lemon zest. Using your fingers, gently pry the skin away from the meat, and insert mixed vegetables. Pour wine over top, and sprinkle with salt and pepper. Cover with plastic wrap, and vent at one end. Microwave on high 8-10 minutes. Let cool slightly, and remove both plastic wrap and skin from breast, leaving cooked vegetables in place.

Preheat barbecue to medium.

Carefully place breast on a square of heavy-duty aluminum foil about three times larger than meat, folding up edges to contain juices. Pour in juices from baking dish, and seal foil by folding over and twisting tightly. Carefully place on barbecue grill, taking care not to puncture foil. Grill 35-45 minutes. Remove from grill, and let cool slightly. Open packet carefully to avoid hot steam.

Orange Ginger Turkey

SERVES 4

When turkey pieces are on sale we stock up, then dream up recipes. This easy dish is equally good served hot with its own sauce on pasta or rice, or cold with potato salad and coleslaw.

– R & W

1/4 cup	butter or margarine	50 ml
1/2 cup	frozen orange juice concentrate, thawed	125 ml
1/4 cup	soy sauce	50 ml
1 tsp	chopped fresh ginger	5 ml
4	turkey breasts or thighs	4

In a large saucepan set over low heat, combine butter, orange juice concentrate, soy sauce, and ginger. Cook 2-3 minutes, stirring occasionally, until heated through. Remove from heat and set aside.

Preheat barbecue to medium-hot.

Place turkey on oiled grill over drip pan. Cook 45-60 minutes, turning occasionally, until fork tender. During the last 15 minutes of cooking, baste turkey with sauce. If serving hot, offer warm sauce on the side.

Sweet and Sour Turkey Drumsticks

SERVES 4

19 fl oz	can sliced pineapple	540 ml
1 Tbsp	cider vinegar	15 ml
1 Tbsp	dark brown sugar	15 ml
1/4 tsp	Tabasco Sauce	1 ml
1 Tbsp	chili powder	15 ml
8	turkey drumsticks or thighs	8

Drain pineapple, and reserve juice. In a large glass cooking dish, mix 1/4 cup (50 ml) pineapple juice, vinegar, brown sugar, Tabasco Sauce, and chili powder. Add turkey, spooning marinade over to coat. Cover and refrigerate 1-2 hours.

Preheat barbecue to medium.

Remove turkey, reserving marinade. Place turkey, bone-side down, on oiled grill. Cover and cook 30-40 minutes. Turn and cook 20-30 minutes more, basting occasionally.

During last 10 minutes of cooking, placed sliced pineapple on grill. Baste with marinade, turn, and baste again, until pineapple begins to brown.

Serve turkey with grilled pineapple slices.

Turkey has taken on a whole new role. When we were kids, we ate roasted turkey at Thanksgiving, Christmas, and Easter, and perhaps once more each year on a special occasion. Now you can enjoy turkey anytime, and you have your choice of dark meat or white, simply by buying either thighs or breasts. This dish is good with a rice pilaf and grilled peppers.

– R & W

VEGGIES: GRILLED & CHILLED

Vegetables at a barbecue used to mean two things — potato salad and coleslaw. Now more and more people are realizing that vegetables (and even fruit) have a rightful place on any respectable backyard grill, and there's no reason for any dedicated vegetarian to shun a barbecue these days. With the popularity of warm salads drizzled with exotic vinaigrettes, fresh vegetables now march regularly from the refrigerator to the heat of a smoking grill. Wonderful salad entrées of charred leeks, asparagus, zucchini, mushrooms, carrots, parsnips, potatoes, peppers, and eggplants are hailed with delight. Marinades made with herb-infused oils and vinegars combined with nut oils, fruit juices, and fresh herbs put a zing into veggies that are grilled quickly and served hot. Gigantic portobello mushrooms can actually be called steak-like when served sizzling with garlic butter and a sprinkling of toasted almonds or sesame seeds. A light spray of cooking oil or brush with herbed oils makes grilling veggies a snap.

Remember, salad veggies and sturdy greens need only be flashed on the grill before they're ready (tender salad greens are not suitable for grilling). Partially pre-cook larger vegetables like potatoes, squash, parsnips, turnip, or carrots using a microwave oven for even speedier results. A wire basket makes grilling vegetables easy and fast, and a basket or perforated enamel tray will keep vegetable pieces from falling through the grill and make turning easy.

And don't turn your back on chilled salads, either, even potato salad and coleslaw. They can often be made in advance, leaving time for your talents to really shine at the grill.

Herb Grilled Vegetables

SERVES 4

This recipe is a winner for vegetarians and omnivores alike. Grilling brings out the great flavour of all kinds of vegetables ,including carrots, zucchini, parsnips, sweet peppers, eggplants, potatoes, mushrooms, asparagus, and spring onions. Serve grilled vegetables with Aïoli (page 41) or Herbed Cheese (page 43).

4	garlic cloves, chopped finely	4
3 Tbsp	canola oil	45 ml
1 Tbsp	balsamic vinegar	15 ml
1 Tbsp	chopped fresh rosemary	15 ml
1 Tbsp	chopped fresh basil	15 ml
	pinch of salt	
	pinch of brown sugar	
1 lb	assorted fresh vegetables	500 g

If you want to cook vegetables on the grill, don't cut them in small pieces or they will fall through. Potatoes and eggplants are best sliced on the diagonal, while carrots, parsnips and zucchini can be halved lengthwise. Quarter peppers, and cook mushrooms whole.

Clean the vegetables and chop or slice them according to whether you're cooking them on the grill, in a basket, or on a perforated tray.

Preheat barbecue to medium-hot.

In a large bowl, mix garlic, oil, vinegar, herbs, salt, and sugar. Toss vegetables well to coat. Place vegetables on oiled grill (or in basket or on oiled tray) and cook 10-15 minutes, basting and turning occasionally until almost tender. Serve slightly charred and piled like a haystack.

Veggie Skewers

Skewering vegetables is an easy way to cook them on the barbecue, and they are great as an accompaniment to any grilled entrée. Use small young cobs of corn when they are in season and at their sweetest.

– R & W

4	small cobs of corn, husked	4
1	small zucchini	1
12	cherry tomatoes	12
8	mushrooms	8
2 Tbsp	melted butter	30 ml
1 Tbsp	canola oil	15 ml
1 tsp	lemon juice	5 ml
1 tsp	dried thyme	5 ml
	salt and freshly ground black pepper	

Cut corn into 1 1/2-inch (3.5-cm) pieces and zucchini into 2-inch (5-cm) chunks.

Preheat barbecue to medium-hot.

If using bamboo skewers, soak them in water for 30 minutes before cooking. Thread corn (piercing through core), zucchini, tomatoes, and mushrooms on skewers. In a small bowl, mix melted butter, oil, lemon juice, and thyme. Baste veggie skewers well, and place on oiled grill. Cook 5-8 minutes, basting and turning frequently, until tender. Season with salt and pepper, and serve hot.

Mediterranean-Style Veggie Pizza

SERVES 2-4

1	medium pizza crust	1
3 Tbsp	herbed oil	45 ml
2 cups	grated mozzarella or feta cheese	500 ml
1	small zucchini, sliced thinly	1
2	medium tomatoes, sliced thinly	2
1	garlic clove, chopped finely	1
2	spring onions, chopped finely	2
8	black olives, pitted and sliced	8
2	sprigs thyme, chopped	2
2 Tbsp	parmesan cheese	30 ml

Almost any vegetables can be used for a vegetarian pizza. If you choose firm vegetables like carrots, cauliflower, or turnips, be sure to blanch them first in boiling salted water for 2-3 minutes. Drain, chill, and pat dry before adding to pizza. We prefer mozzarella or feta cheese, but you can use your own favourite.

– R & W

Preheat barbecue to hot.

Brush pizza crust with herbed oil, and place on perforated pizza pan. Spread with cheese, zucchini, tomatoes, garlic, onions, and olives. Scatter fresh thyme and parmesan cheese on top, and bake in closed barbecue for 10-15 minutes.

Hodge Podge

This traditional Maritime dish, introduced to us by our friend Bea, is best made with freshly harvested new vegetables. We've adapted the recipe for the barbecue by cooking the vegetables in foil, which seals in their flavourful juices. We often make a full meal of Hodge Podge.

— R & W

1/2 lb	small new potatoes	250 g
1/4 lb	green beans	125 g
1/4 lb	baby carrots	125 g
1/2 lb	fresh peas, shelled	250 g
1 tsp	salt	5 ml
1/4 tsp	freshly ground black pepper	1 ml
1 Tbsp	butter, softened	15 ml
3/4 cup	cream (18% or more)	175 ml

Cut potatoes and carrots into bite-sized pieces, and halve beans. Preheat barbecue to medium-hot.

Place vegetables on a sheet of heavy-duty aluminum foil that's large enough to fold into a packet. If you have too many vegetables to work with comfortably, make two packets. Sprinkle vegetables with salt and pepper, and dot with butter. Wrap foil loosely, but seal tightly.

Place packet on grill for 20-25 minutes or until vegetables are tender, turning once. Before removing packet from grill, carefully cut a slit in the foil, and pour in cream. Leave on grill for 2 minutes to heat cream through. Pour contents of packet into large bowl. Season with extra salt and pepper, if necessary, and serve at once.

Lemon Dill Beets

When you have a passion for a certain food, you will always find an oppertunity to cook it. Imagine my delight at discovering a recipe for beets on the barbecue. Heaven.

– W

8	medium-sized whole beets, peeled and topped	8
1 Tbsp	melted butter	15 ml
1 Tbsp	lemon juice	15 ml
1 1/2 tsp	chopped fresh dill	7 ml

Preheat barbecue to medium-hot.

Place prepared beets on a large piece of aluminum foil. Drizzle with butter, lemon, and dill. Fold foil into a packet, sealing edges.

Place on grill and cook, turning frequently, for 45 minutes, or until beets are tender.

Grilled Corn on the Cob

Try this trick to make a little butter go a long way. Remove the top from a large, empty fruit juice can. Fill the can halfway with boiling water, and add 1/2 pound (125 g) butter to the water. Place can over low heat on grill, and let butter melt. Carefully push each cooked corn cob into the butter and water mixture. As the corn is pushed into the liquid, the melted butter coats it as the water rises. Carefully lift the cob from the can, letting excess butter drip back into the hot water. Repeat with as many cobs as possible, until the butter is used up. Add more butter when necessary.

When the barbecue is hot and ready to go, try grilling fresh corn on the cob instead of boiling it. It makes a succulent summertime treat. For an extra boost of flavour, serve corn with Herb Butter (page 31).

– R & W

12	ears fresh corn, in husks	12
	butter	
	salt	
	freshly ground black pepper	
	non-plastic twist ties or fine wire	

Preheat barbecue to medium-hot.

Carefully open each ear of corn and remove as much of the silk as possible. Rewrap the husks and tie ends with non-plastic twist ties or wire to keep ears sealed. Soak in a pail of cold water for 15-20 minutes. Remove corn from water, and place on barbecue grill. Close lid, and cook 8-10 minutes, turning regularly. Don't worry if the husks char. Remove corn carefully, let rest for 5 minutes, then trim stalk ends. Remove leaves, and serve with plenty of butter, salt and pepper.

Eggplant Bruschetta

Delightful as an appetizer or first course, bruschetta makes a wonderful light lunch, much like mini pizza.

– R & W

1	medium eggplant	1
	salt	
1	sweet red or yellow pepper	1
1/2 cup	olive oil	125 ml
1 tsp	minced fresh garlic	5 ml
1 tsp	balsamic vinegar	5 ml
1/4 cup	chopped fresh parsley	50 ml
2 Tbsp	chopped fresh basil	30 ml
	salt and freshly ground black pepper	
8	thick slices Italian or French bread	8
1	garlic clove, peeled and halved	1

Cut eggplant in 1/2-inch (1-cm) slices.

Preheat barbecue to medium-hot.

Sprinkle eggplant slices with salt, and drain on paper towel for 30 minutes. Rinse with cold water and pat dry.

Meanwhile, char the pepper on the oiled grill, turning frequently, until well blackened. Remove from grill, cover with a towel. Let sit 10 minutes, and then remove blackened skin. Cut in half, and remove seeds and stem. Slice in long strips, and set aside.

Brush eggplant with olive oil, and cook on oiled grill, turning frequently, 4 minutes per side, until tender and browned. Remove from grill, chop, and, in a medium-sized bowl, mix it with pepper strips, 1 Tbsp (15 ml) oil, garlic, vinegar, parsley, and basil. Season to taste with salt and pepper, and set aside.

Grill bread slices on both sides, watching closely, until toasted. Remove from grill, and rub with cut garlic clove. Spoon a large dollop of eggplant mixture on each slice of toast, and serve while still warm.

Eggplant Kebabs

SERVES 8

2	eggplants	2
3 Tbsp	tarragon vinegar	45 ml
3 Tbsp	herbed olive oil	45 ml
1	garlic clove, chopped	1
1/4 tsp	salt	1 ml
1/2 tsp	Dijon mustard	2 ml
1 Tbsp	chopped fresh parsley	15 ml
	dash of hot sauce	
1 Tbsp	honey	15 ml
1 tsp	chopped fresh oregano	5 ml
	oregano to garnish	

Preheat barbecue to medium-hot.

Peel eggplants, cut in half, then cut into 1-inch (2.5-cm) cubes.

In a large bowl, combine remaining ingredients except garnish. Add eggplant cubes and toss. Let sit for 15 minutes, stirring occasionally.

Thread cubes onto skewers and place on rack over grill for 15 minutes, turning occasionally. Serve with barbecued steaks or chops, and garnish the plates with oregano.

My father-in-law introduced me to eggplant 30 years ago. Most Saturdays he visited the supermarket produce department just before closing. He would offer the manager a pittance for leftover vegetables and fruit, knowing it would spoil over the weekend. He'd then come and share his bounty with me, a habit that made me scramble for new recipes.
– W

Grilled New Potatoes

Small potatoes are available all year round — if you're prepared to pay the price. We still wait for the first new baby potatoes of summer, and we particularly enjoy them cooked on the barbecue.

– R & W

6	new red or white potatoes, halved	6
1 Tbsp	canola oil	15 ml
2	garlic cloves, chopped	2
1 tsp	paprika	5 ml
1/2 tsp	dried rosemary, crushed	2 ml
	salt and freshly ground black pepper	

Preheat barbecue to medium-hot.

Place potatoes in glass baking dish, drizzle with canola oil, and mix to coat well. Sprinkle with chopped garlic, paprika, and rosemary. Cover with waxed paper, and microwave on high for 8-10 minutes, until just tender.

Transfer potatoes to oiled grill, cut-sides down. Close lid and cook 3-4 minutes. Turn and grill 2-3 minutes more, until browned. Serve hot.

Baked Potatoes with Garlic Cream

SERVES 4

4	baking potatoes, scrubbed and patted dry	4
	herbed vegetable oil	
1/2 cup	sour cream	125 ml
2 tsp	grated onion	10 ml
2	garlic cloves, minced	2
1/2 cup	grated cheddar cheese	125 ml
2 Tbsp	chopped fresh chives	30 ml

When I was a kid, my brothers and I used to cook potatoes in an open fire on the beach by tossing them directly into the coals. When they were done, we peeled away the burnt skin. We had no butter, salt, or pepper, but they were a taste treat we still talk about fondly.
– W

Preheat barbecue to medium-hot.

Pierce potatoes in several places with a fork or skewer. Rub with herbed oil (we prefer garlic for this recipe), wrap individually in a double thickness of aluminum foil, and bake on grill 45-60 minutes, turning occasionally, until soft.

Meanwhile, in a small bowl, combine sour cream, onion, garlic, and cheese.

When potatoes are baked, carefully remove from foil. Cut an X in each potato, and squeeze gently, or "blossom," to open. Spoon a dollop of sour cream mixture on each potato, and sprinkle with chives. Put the remaining cream on the table for second helpings.

Smoked Salmon and Dill Potatoes

SERVES 4

When Ross and I want something quick and tasty for a light supper or lunch, we often turn to the "lowly" potato. Baked potatoes are so versatile they can be stuffed with anything from broccoli and cheese to exotic items like poached eggs and hollandaise sauce. This recipe is one of our favourites.

– W

4	baking potatoes, scrubbed and patted dry	4
	vegetable oil	
1/2 cup	sour cream	125 ml
1 tsp	chopped fresh dill	5 ml
1 tsp	lemon juice	5 ml
1/2 lb	smoked salmon, chopped	250 g
	capers, to garnish	

Preheat barbecue to medium-hot.

Pierce potatoes in several places with a fork or skewer. Rub with oil, wrap individually in double thickness of aluminum foil, and bake on grill 45-60 minutes, turning occasionally, until soft.

Meanwhile, in a small bowl, combine sour cream, dill, and lemon juice.

When potatoes are baked, carefully remove from foil. Cut an X in each potato, and squeeze gently to open. Place a generous amount of salmon on each, and spoon a dollop of cream on top. Garnish with capers. Put the remaining cream and smoked salmon on the table for second helpings.

Sweet Potato Salad

SERVES 4

1 Tbsp	sesame oil	15 ml
2 tsp	soy sauce	10 ml
	juice and zest of 1 lemon	
3	garlic cloves, finely chopped	3
2	large sweet potatoes, cut in 1-inch (2.5-cm) cubes	2
2 Tbsp	vegetable oil	30 ml
1	large onion, sliced	1
1 Tbsp	chopped fresh thyme	15 ml
2 Tbsp	toasted sesame seeds	30 ml
2	sliced spring onions	2

My mother loved pale yellow yams, which are often sold as sweet potatoes but do not even belong to the same family. This recipe calls for sweet potatoes, the orange-fleshed tubers we commonly see in our markets.

– W

Preheat barbecue to medium.

In a large bowl, combine sesame oil, soy sauce, lemon juice and zest, and 1 tsp (5 ml) of the chopped garlic. Set aside.

On a large piece of heavy aluminum foil, combine sweet potatoes, vegetable oil, onion, remaining garlic, and thyme. Fold and seal foil. Place on grill, and cook 30 minutes, turning occasionally, until sweet potatoes are tender. Remove from heat, carefully open foil, and let cool slightly.

Add cooked vegetables to dressing with toasted sesame seeds and onions. Toss to coat. Serve slightly warm, or refrigerate for up to one day and serve cold.

Ginger Maple Sweet Potatoes

SERVES 8

Fresh ginger and maple syrup turn sweet potatoes from ordinary to special. These are a great addition to the barbecued turkey at Thanksgiving or Christmas.

– R & W

4	sweet potatoes, cut in 1/2-inch (1-cm) slices	4
1/4 cup	butter	50 ml
2 Tbsp	maple syrup	30 ml
1 tsp	grated fresh ginger	5 ml

Preheat barbecue to medium-hot.

Arrange sweet potato slices in a glass baking dish, and partially cook for 6 minutes in microwave until slightly tender.

In a small saucepan, melt butter, maple syrup and ginger. Cook 1-2 minutes.

Spread sweet potato slices on cookie sheet, and baste with butter mixture. Transfer slices to oiled grill. Cook 5-10 minutes, turning and basting frequently, until tender.

Herbed Maple Parsnips

SERVES 4

Parsnips are often overlooked, but we love them — boiled, mashed, or baked. We promise you your family and guests will have a whole new respect for them once they taste parsnips cooked on the grill.

– W

4	parsnips, washed but not peeled	4
	herbed olive oil	
	salt	
	maple syrup	

This recipe works equally well with any variety of winter squash. Cut the squash lengthwise, and scoop out the seeds and pulp. Cut the halves in 1/2-inch (1-cm) slices. Cook as described, until tender.

Preheat barbecue to medium-hot.

Remove stem ends from parsnips, and slice lengthwise into 1/4-inch (5-mm) slices. Brush with herbed olive oil (or plain olive oil if you prefer), and sprinkle with salt.

Place parsnips on oiled grill, cover, and cook for 5 minutes per side, until tender and lightly browned. Brush with maple syrup, and cook for 30 seconds more on each side.

Zucchini Roast

If your neighbour offers you fresh zucchini, cross your fingers and hope they are very small, about 5 inches (12 cm) long. Too often we aren't given zucchini, or courgettes, until they have to be transported by wheelbarrow. Those are good to grate and use in muffins and cake, but the small ones are the real gems. This recipe makes a wonderful accompaniment to any grilled meat, especially lamb.

– R & W

8	small zucchini, ends removed	8
1 tsp	lemon zest	5 ml
1 tsp	finely chopped fresh mint	5 ml
1 tsp	finely chopped fresh oregano	5 ml
2	bay leaves	2
1/2 tsp	salt	2 ml
2 Tbsp	white wine	30 ml
2 Tbsp	lemon juice	30 ml
4 Tbsp	olive oil	60 ml

Pierce zucchini in several places with a fork or skewer.

In a large bowl, mix together the remaining ingredients. Add zucchini, coating well. Cover and marinate 4-5 hours, mixing occasionally.

Preheat barbecue to medium-hot.

Remove zucchini from marinade, and place on oiled grill. Cook 4-5 minutes on each side, turning frequently and basting with marinade.

Ratatouille Toast

5 Tbsp	herbed oil or olive oil	75 ml
1 tsp	finely chopped garlic	5 ml
1	mild onion, sliced thinly into rings	1
1	yellow pepper, sliced thinly	1
1	red pepper, sliced thinly	1
1	orange pepper, sliced thinly	1
1 Tbsp	chopped fresh basil	15 ml
1	loaf French bread	1
1 cup	grated Swiss cheese	250 ml

This colourful appetizer will delight your guests — and its simplicity will make the cook happy too. Although it doesn't have all the ingredients of a traditional ratatouille, Ross thinks it's close enough to bear the name. It is great as the first course of an elegant sit-down dinner or at an easygoing backyard affair.

– W

Preheat barbecue to medium.

Heat oil in a large frying pan over medium-high heat for 1-2 minutes. Add garlic and onion, lower heat to medium, and sauté for 3-5 minutes, until softened but not browned. Remove onion and garlic from pan, and add peppers and basil. Cook 3-5 minutes, until just tender but not browned. Return onion and garlic to pan, and mix well. Remove from heat.

Cut bread diagonally in 1-inch (2.5-cm) slices. Place slices on grill, and toast 2-3 minutes. Turn and brush with herbed oil. Remove from grill, and top with pepper mixture. Sprinkle with grated cheese, and return to grill for 2-4 minutes, until cheese is bubbly.

Roasted Rainbow Vegetables

SERVES 4

To prevent onion slices from separating into rings when grilling, place them flat on a cutting board and insert three toothpicks through the sides of each slice.

The wonderful array of fresh sweet peppers available now often resembles a rainbow. Don't stop at three colours — try them all!
– R & W

3	sweet peppers (red, green, and yellow)	3
1	large red onion	1
1/4 cup	olive oil	50 ml
1 Tbsp	cider vinegar	15 ml
1/2 tsp	dried thyme	2 ml
	salt and freshly ground black pepper	

Quarter and seed peppers, and cut onion in 1/2-inch (1-cm) slices. Place peppers and onion slices in large glass bowl. In a small jar, shake together olive oil and cider vinegar. Drizzle over vegetables. Sprinkle with thyme, salt, and pepper, and set aside.

Preheat barbecue to medium-hot.

Place vegetables on oiled grill. Close lid, and cook 7-8 minutes. Turn vegetables, and cook a further 8-10 minutes until browned and sizzling. Serve hot.

Eggplant Stuffed Sweet Peppers

SERVES 4

Sweet peppers all start out being green. As they ripen on the vine, they change colour according to variety: red, yellow, orange, and even purple. Brightly coloured peppers are sweeter than green peppers, but all will mellow and sweeten in flavour when cooked.

– R & W

4	sweet peppers	4
1	medium sized eggplant, cut in 1/4-inch (5-mm) slices	1
	salt	
1/4 cup	olive oil	50 ml
1 cup	breadcrumbs	250 ml
2	garlic cloves, minced	2
1/2 cup	grated parmesan cheese	125 ml
1/4 cup	chopped fresh parsley	50 ml
1 Tbsp	chopped fresh basil	15 ml
1	egg, beaten	1
	salt and freshly ground black pepper	

Slice tops from peppers, and remove and discard seeds and core. Set peppers and tops aside.

Lightly salt eggplant slices, and set aside to drain on paper towels for about 30 minutes. Rinse with cold water, and pat dry. Chop coarsely. Heat oil in a large frying pan over high heat. Sauté eggplant for 5 minutes, until tender and browned. Remove from pan, place on cutting board, and chop finely.

In a large bowl, mix eggplant with breadcrumbs, garlic, parmesan, parsley, and basil. Add beaten egg, salt, and pepper, and mix well.

Preheat barbecue to medium-hot.

Stuff pepper shells with eggplant mixture. Place tops on peppers and fasten with toothpicks. Cook peppers on oiled grill on a covered barbecue for 1 hour, turning occasionally.

Peppers will become charred. You can remove the blackened skins before serving, or you can scrape the skin away as you eat. But do remember to remove the toothpicks!

Use the same number of toothpicks to secure each pepper, so you will know how many to remove. This will prevent diners from biting into a stray toothpick.

Bean-Hole Beans

SERVES 8-12

1 lb	soldier or navy beans, soaked overnight	500 g
1	onion, chopped	1
1/4 lb	salt pork, cut into 1/2-inch (1-cm) cubes	125 g
2 tsp	dry mustard	10 ml
3 Tbsp	brown sugar	45 ml
1/2 tsp	freshly ground black pepper	2 ml
2 Tbsp	butter	30 ml
1/2 cup	molasses	125 ml
1/4 tsp	salt	1 ml

This recipe goes back to the days of the lumber camps, and the method works very well if you're planning an outdoor dinner about a day and a half away. Being aware of the dangers of underground fires, we prefer to bake our beans in a hole on the beach above the high-water line and well away from tree roots. Use a heavy iron or crockery pot with a tightly fitting lid. You will also need a large piece of sheet metal to cover the hole.

– R & W

Dig a hole about twice as wide as the pot you will be using and as deep as the pot plus an extra foot (30 cm) to allow room for the coals on the sides, bottom, and top. Build a large fire in the hole, adding to the wood from time to time to ensure plenty of glowing coals.

Meanwhile, put all the ingredients in the bean pot. Add enough water to just cover the beans. Securely close the pot.

When the fire has died down slightly, remove about half the embers, and place the pot down into the remaining coals. Quickly shovel the reserved hot coals around and on top of the pot. Cover the hole with the sheet metal and a heavy layer of sand. Let sit for 24 hours.

Carefully shovel off the sand, and remove the sheet metal. Lift out the pot, and enjoy a new taste delight.

We like to have a small bonfire going at this time so we can roast hot dogs and sausages on sticks to accompany the beans.

Parsley and Cheese Stuffed Onions

SERVES 4

Stuffed onions make a nice accompaniment to main dishes, or they can be served on their own as a light lunch with a side salad and warm bread. We like to use local onions in the late summer and fall, when they're crisp and sweet. Mild Spanish or Vidalia varieties are good in the spring.

– R & W

4	large onions, skins removed	4
1/2 cup	breadcrumbs	125 ml
1 Tbsp	chopped fresh parsley	15 ml
1 tsp	lemon zest	5 ml
	white wine	
	salt	
	freshly ground black pepper	
2 Tbsp	grated Swiss cheese	30 ml

Preheat barbecue to medium-hot.

Cut a slice from the top of each onion, and scoop out the flesh, leaving two or three layers of shell. Chop onion flesh finely, and combine with breadcrumbs, parsley, lemon zest, and enough white wine to moisten. Season to taste with salt and pepper.

Using a small spoon, fill the onion shells with stuffing, and wrap individually in heavy foil. Place on grill, and bake for 45-60 minutes, until tender, turning occasionally. Carefully open packets to reveal onion tops, and sprinkle with grated cheese. Serve hot.

Grilled Fennel and Potato Salad

SERVES 4

4	medium potatoes, scrubbed and cut in 1/4-inch (5-mm) slices	4
1	large fennel bulb, cut in 1/4-inch (5-mm) slices	1
	olive oil	
1 cup	mayonnaise	250 ml
2 Tbsp	whipping cream	30 ml
1	garlic clove, minced	1
2	green onions, chopped finely	2
2 tsp	honey	10 ml
1/4 tsp	dry mustard	1 ml
	salt and freshly ground black pepper	
	fresh basil leaves to garnish	

This salad can be served warm, or you can prepare it ahead of time and serve it chilled. Grilling the vegetables adds a whole new dimension to potato salad.

– R & W

Preheat barbecue to medium-hot.

Thread potato and fennel slices onto separate skewers. Brush with oil. Grill potato slices on oiled grill 3-5 minutes per side, until tender. Grill fennel for 2 minutes per side. Both should be browned and tender when pierced with a fork. Cool slightly, and cut each fennel slice in half. Arrange potato slices in a large bowl with fennel on top.

In a medium-sized bowl, mix remaining ingredients, seasoning to taste with salt and pepper. Drizzle over potatoes and fennel. Garnish with fresh basil leaves.

Tomato and Bread Salad

SERVES 4

This Italian dish is a unique blend of vegetables, fish, and bread. As unlikely as it might seem, it is absolutely perfect with barbecued lamb dishes. The saltiness of the anchovies, the sweetness of the tomatoes, and the bite of the onions act as the perfect foil to the richness of lamb.

– R & W

2	thick slices dry bread, cut in 1-inch (2.5-cm) cubes	2
3/4 cup	tomato juice	175 ml
1/2	small yellow pepper, diced	1/2
1	small red onion, diced	1
1	garlic clove, chopped finely	1
3	anchovy fillets, chopped	3
1 Tbsp	capers, drained and chopped	15 ml
1/3 cup	olive oil	75 ml
1 Tbsp	apple cider vinegar	15 ml
1/2 cup	thinly sliced cucumber	125 ml
1	large tomato, diced	1

Place bread cubes in large bowl. Pour tomato juice over bread, and let stand until liquid is absorbed. In another bowl, combine diced pepper, onion, garlic, anchovies, capers, oil, and vinegar. Mix well. Pour over bread and mix well. Add cucumber slices and diced tomato, stir, and serve at once.

Balsamic Vegetable Salad

SERVES 8

When we were growing up, there was usually a bottle of white vinegar in the cupboard. We were introduced to malt vinegar with our first fish and chips. Now there are new vinegars being introduced to our supermarkets all the time. Balsamic vinegar is almost "old hat," but we still like it.

– R & W

3	peppers, cut in chunks	3
2	small zucchini, sliced thickly on the diagonal	2
1	medium yellow summer squash, cut in chunks	1
4	leeks, cleaned and sliced lengthways	4
16	button mushrooms	16
12	cherry tomatoes	12
1/4 cup	olive oil	50 ml
2 Tbsp	chopped fresh thyme	30 ml
2	garlic cloves, minced	2
2 Tbsp	balsamic vinegar	30 ml
	salt	
	freshly ground black pepper	

Preheat barbecue to hot.

Thread all the vegetable pieces except the tomatoes onto metal skewers; set aside separate skewers for the tomatoes, which take less time to cook.

In a small bowl, mix olive oil, thyme, and garlic.

Place skewers on oiled grill, baste vegetables with seasoned oil, and lower heat to medium. Grill, turning and basting occasionally, until cooked. Zucchini, peppers, squash, leeks, and mushrooms should cook for 8-10 minutes. Tomatoes will take only 2-3 minutes. When just tender and browned, remove from grill, and slide vegetables off skewers into a large bowl. Drizzle with balsamic vinegar, and toss well. Add salt and pepper to taste.

Grilled Endive

This simple but elegant recipe is perfect for serving with any meat or fish dish.

– R & W

4	heads Belgian endive	4
	herbed olive oil	
	salt	

Preheat barbecue to medium-hot.

Wash endives, and slice in half lengthwise. Rinse again to remove any grit, being careful not to separate leaves from stem. Brush both sides with herbed olive oil, and sprinkle lightly with salt.

Place endives on an open, oiled grill, and cook 3-5 minutes per side, or until stem ends are tender and leaves are light brown and crisp.

Nibbles, Drinks & Sweet Endings

There is more to a barbecue than just meat and potatoes. Bread, biscuits, pizza, nibbles, desserts, and beverages to wet your whistle complete the meal. There really is little you can't accomplish with your barbecue. Consider it a portable, gas-fired oven outdoors, and let your imagination run wild. When cooking a prime rib, add Yorkshire puddings to accompany the roast. Think of your barbecue as your gas range, and you'll never be too old to ride it. You won't be thrown, if you can accurately judge the temperature of the oven and the best height from the heat to place food. All it takes is practice and experience.

For baked food like Yorkshire Puddings, rolls, and pizza, sit the baking pan across two masonry bricks placed on the grill to discourage scorching on the bottom and encourage even baking. Place them on their sides to elevate the baking pan or sheet two inches (5 cm), and turn them on edge to raise the pan four inches (10 cm) above the grill.

Desserts from the grill are the natural extension of any barbecue. Before the heat dies down, quickly toast pound cake and fruit slices for a heavenly repast. A drizzle of maple syrup or melted cheese on grilled fruit is wonderful. Those melted marshmallow and chocolate treats you enjoyed as a kid around a campfire can all be adapted to barbecue cooking. Let your imagination be your inspiration.

Garlic Fan Rolls

SERVES 6-8

This a quick and easy way to produce delicious "homemade" garlic bread on the grill. Read the package instructions carefully, as some "ready-to-serve" rolls may heat through more quickly than "brown-and-serve" rolls.

– R & W

6-8	brown-and-serve rolls, split	6-8
1/4 lb	butter, softened	125 g
1	garlic clove, crushed	1
1/8 tsp	salt	5 ml

Preheat barbecue to medium.

Place rolls on double thickness of heavy-duty aluminium foil. In a small saucepan, melt butter with garlic and salt. Brush generously between, and on top of rolls, and wrap securely in foil. Grill for 10-12 minutes, turn, and cook 10 minutes more, until browned.

Foiled Poppy-Seed Loaf

SERVES 6-8

The first time I tasted poppy seeds was in this bread at a childhood picnic in the San Juan Islands, in Washington state. This foil-wrapped bread is delicious and easily prepared on the grill.

– R

1	loaf white bread, unsliced	1
1/2 cup	melted butter	125 ml
2	garlic cloves, chopped finely	2
3 Tbsp	poppy seeds	45 ml
1 Tbsp	dried thyme	15 ml

Preheat barbecue to medium-hot.

Cut loaf in half from end to end and in 4 crosswise to make 8 pieces. Place on double thickness of aluminum foil, and brush completely with melted butter and garlic. Sprinkle with poppy seeds and thyme, and close foil tightly to form a sealed packet.

Place packet on grill, and close lid. Grill 10-12 minutes, turning frequently, until butter sizzles. Remove from heat, and carefully open foil to serve hot.

Spicy Grilled Camembert

SERVES 4

This recipe brings a whole new meaning to grilled cheese. It's a great appetizer and is easily prepared while dinner is cooking.

– R & W

1 Tbsp	olive or canola oil	15 ml
1 tsp	lemon juice	5 ml
1/4 tsp	salt	1 ml
1/4 tsp	dried thyme	1 ml
1/2 tsp	chili powder	2 ml
1	small round Camembert or Brie cheese	1

Preheat barbecue to medium-hot.

Mix oil, lemon juice, salt, thyme, and chili into a thin paste, and spread all over whole cheese. Place on grill and heat 2-3 minutes on each side. Serve hot with toast wedges or crackers.

Cheesy Grilled Polenta ~good~

SERVES 6-8

I first ate polenta when I worked in a town with a large Italian community. It's especially delicious when finished on the grill.

– R

3 cups	chicken broth	750 ml
1 cup	cornmeal	250 ml
2 Tbsp	butter	30 ml
1 Tbsp	chopped fresh parsley	15 ml
1/3 cup	grated parmesan cheese	75 ml
	freshly ground black pepper	
2 Tbsp	olive oil	30 ml
	extra parmesan, to serve	

In a large saucepan over medium heat, bring broth to a boil. Gradually stir in cornmeal, and simmer 5-6 minutes, stirring frequently, until mixture thickens, Remove from heat, and stir in butter, parsley, parmesan, and pepper. Spoon into a lightly greased 8-inch (20-cm) square baking dish, spreading evenly. Set aside to cool for several hours.

Preheat barbecue to ~~medium~~ hot.

Turn polenta out of dish, and cut in 2 1/2-inch (6-cm) square pieces. Brush with oil and grill for 2 minutes per side. Sprinkle with extra parmesan, and serve hot as a side dish or appetizer.

 messy on bbq

Bannock

This pioneer-style biscuit can be made over a campfire, on your barbecue, or on your stove. Bannock is best when fresh-baked, with butter and jam, or as a savor accompaniment with roasting garlic.

– R & W

2 cups	flour	500 ml
1/2 tsp	salt	2 ml
2 tsp	baking powder	10 ml
2/3 cup	cold water	150 ml
2 Tbsp	oil, butter, or bacon fat	30 ml

Preheat barbecue to medium.

In a large bowl, combine dry ingredients. Add water and oil, mixing well. Knead dough until well combined. Roll or pat to fit frying pan, and score in wedges. Melt oil, butter, or bacon fat in pan, and add dough. Cook 10-15 minutes, turning once. Alternatively, you can cook bannock directly on the oiled grill. Bannock should sound hollow when tapped.

Bannock can also be baked in a conventional oven at 400°F (200°C) for about 15 or 20 minutes.

Roasting garlic diffuses its strong, sharp flavour, leaving it sweet and mellow. To roast garlic on the barbecue, cut 1/4 inch (5 mm) off the tops of several bulbs of firm, fresh garlic, exposing the cloves. Rub the tops of the bulbs with olive oil, sprinkle lightly with salt, and place in a baking dish with a sprig of rosemary. (We use a clay dish meant to sit under a plant pot.) Place directly on medium-hot grill and bake 30 minutes, or until nicely browned. Garlic should be soft and easily squeezed out of its skin.

Barbecued Yorkshire Pudding

SERVES 12

This recipe makes 12 large muffin-sized Yorkshires. Serve them hot right from the barbecue with lots of beef gravy. Recipe can be halved.

If you wish to make these delicious puds sans roast, simply substitute canola or olive oil for the beef drippings. Yorkshire Puddings are equally suitable served with roast chicken or grilled vegetables.

– R & W

12 tsp	beef drippings	60 ml
4	eggs	4
2 cups	milk	500 ml
2 cups	all-purpose flour	500 ml
1 tsp	salt	5 ml

For best results, have your eggs and milk at room temperature. If you are serving Yorkshire Puddings with a roast, have the ingredients measured and ready, along with a large 12-cup muffin pan, before you remove the roast from the spit.

Set bricks on the grill to elevate the muffin pan about 4 inches (10 cm). Preheat barbecue to hot.

Place 1 tsp (5 ml) hot drippings from the rotisserie drip pan into each muffin cup. (We often use a turkey baster for this job.)

In a large glass measuring cup or bowl, beat eggs with an electric hand mixer for 30 seconds until frothy. Add milk and beat for 15-20 seconds more. Mix in flour and salt, beating for at least 2 minutes more, until batter is creamy and smooth. Place muffin pan on the grill for about 1 minute, until drippings or oil are sizzling. Quickly pour batter into cups, filling them almost to the top. Place on bricks, close barbecue lid, and bake undisturbed for 25-30 minutes. Don't open the lid to peek for at least 20 minutes. Puddings should be risen and ready after 30 minutes. Don't over-bake Yorkshire Puddings. They should be crusty outside and soft and slightly moist inside.

Lemonade Spritzer

If you're tired of ho-hum lemonade, give this fizzy treat a try. Sit back on the veranda in that wicker rocker, and y'all will feel like Miss Scarlett. Add a splash of vodka to turn this drink from soft to hard.

– R & W

12 oz	can frozen lemonade concentrate	341 ml
1 cup	cold water	250 ml
3 Tbsp	lemon juice	45 ml
3 cups	club soda, chilled	750 ml
2 cups	ice cubes	500 ml
	fresh lemon slices and mint sprigs for garnish	

In a large pitcher, combine lemonade concentrate and water, and stir until concentrate is thawed. Add lemon juice, soda, and 2 cups (500 ml) ice cubes. Fill glasses, and top with a lemon slice, split slightly to fit over the rim of the glass, and a sprig of mint.

Fruit Twist

Prepare this drink as is, and the whole family can enjoy it. Add rum, and it's a fruit drink with a twist for adults only.

– R & W

3 cups	unsweetened pineapple juice, chilled	750 ml
2	ripe bananas	2
4 tsp	honey	20 ml
1	lime, freshly squeezed	1
1 cup	crushed ice	250 ml
4 oz	rum (optional)	125 ml
	lime, quartered	
	sugar	

In a blender, combine pineapple juice, bananas, honey, lime juice, and crushed ice. Blend until smooth.

Rub rims of glasses with quartered lime and dip in a saucer of sugar. Fill glasses with punch, and serve cold.

Iced Raspberry Beer

SERVES 2

Raspberries grow in the field next to our summer home on the Kingston Peninsula. When we want to make this drink, we simply pick berries, take them to the kitchen, and proceed with the recipe. Life is good.

– R & W

3 cups	fresh or frozen raspberries	750 ml
2	lemons freshly squeezed	2
1/2 cup	powdered sugar	125 ml
	crushed ice	
12 oz	beer	341 ml

In a blender, pulse raspberries until crushed and juicy. Add lemon juice, and blend well.

Rub rims of glasses with squeezed lemon halves, and dip rims in a saucer of sugar. Fill each glass halfway with crushed ice. Pour in raspberry juice to cover ice, and top with chilled beer. Serve at once.

Olde English Punch

This drink looks refreshing even before you savour it. We like to use strawberries or raspberries, but any berries can be added to bring extra colour to the cool green depths of this punch.

– R & W

4 cups	lemonade	1 l
2 cups	ginger ale	500 ml
2 cups	tonic water	500 ml
2 cups	soda water	500 ml
3/4 cup	orange juice	175 ml
1/4 cup	freshly squeezed lemon juice	50 ml
3	sprigs fresh mint, bruised	3
	peel of 1/2 cucumber	
1	unpeeled Granny Smith apple, cored and sliced	1
	strawberries to garnish	

Combine ingredients in a large pitcher, and mix with ice before serving.

Sangria

Popular in the late sixties and early seventies, this drink is making a comeback as more and more people entertain in their gardens and back yards. If you were too young to have enjoyed it the first time around, you're not too young now.

– R & W

1	large orange	1
1	large lemon	1
1/8 tsp	cinnamon	.5 ml
1/8 tsp	nutmeg	.5 ml
1/4 cup	brandy	50 ml
3 cups	red Bordeaux wine	750 ml
	sugar	
1 cup	club soda, chilled	250 ml
	ice cubes	
	orange slices, to garnish	

Cut 2 thick slices from middles of orange and lemon. Set aside.

Squeeze juice from remaining orange and lemon into a large pitcher, catching and discarding seeds. Add spices, brandy, wine, and sugar to taste. Mix well, and stir in orange and lemon slices. Cover, and refrigerate for 1 hour. Before serving, add chilled soda water. Add ice to tall glasses, and fill with sangria. Garnish with orange slice.

Citrus Wine

A refreshing drink to have ready for the first time you invite new neighbours or co-workers for a backyard barbecue. It's pleasantly light and goes well with any appetizer, especially during what Ross calls a "whine and cheese break."

– W

2 cups	orange juice, freshly squeezed	500 ml
1 cup	frozen lemonade concentrate, thawed	250 ml
1 cup	Grand Marnier or other orange liqueur	250 ml
3 cups	dry white wine	750 ml
4 cups	club soda, chilled	1 l
	ice	
	orange slices, to garnish	

In a large pitcher or punch bowl, combine orange juice, lemonade concentrate, orange liqueur, and wine. Just before serving, add soda and ice. Stir well, and serve in ice-filled wine glasses, garnished with orange slices.

Iced Coffee

We buy our coffee from two entrepreneurs who roast, blend, and grind beans on their premises. We enjoy water from our own bubbling spring, and each morning our guests rave about our coffee. It just goes to show that if you start with the best possible ingredients, you will end up with superior results.

– R & W

1 cup	sugar	250 ml
1 1/2 cups	whole milk	375 ml
1 tsp	vanilla (or 1 vanilla bean)	5 ml
1 1/2 cups	cold coffee	375 ml
1 cup	whipping cream	250 ml
	whipped cream, unsweetened	

In a heavy-based saucepan over medium-high heat, combine sugar, milk, and vanilla. Bring to a boil, stirring until sugar is dissolved. Remove from heat, and let cool.

In a large bowl, combine cooled milk mixture, coffee, and 3/4 cup (175 ml) whipping cream. Pour into shallow metal pan. Place in freezer until partially frozen. Return iced coffee mixture to bowl and stir. Whip remaining cream until soft peaks form. Fill tall glasses two-thirds full with coffee mixture, and top with whipped cream. Serve immediately.

Iced Sun Tea

If removed in long, fine strips, citrus zest can be slightly cooked in a light sugar syrup for 20-30 minutes, drained, and allowed to set or harden. It can then be rolled in granulated sugar, left to dry, and used in dessert recipes as a flavourful topping or accent.

My introduction to iced tea occurred in South Carolina, when friends offered me tea after a day of sailing. As a Maritimer, I anticipated a steaming "cuppa." The tall chilled glass topped with lemon wasn't what I expected, but it was wonderful, and I've loved iced tea ever since. This is also a Southern recipe, great for back yards or on the boat.

– W

4	tea bags	4
4 cups	water	1 litre
1/4 cup	sugar (optional)	50 ml
1/4 cup	grapefruit juice	50 ml
1/4 cup	lemon juice	50 ml
1/4 cup	orange juice	50 ml
	lemon slices and mint leaves, to garnish	

Combine tea bags and water in a tall, clear pitcher, and cover. Set in direct sunlight (on deck or windowsill) for 2 hours, or until steeped. Remove tea bags. Add sugar (or allow guests to sweeten their own). Stir in juices, and serve in tall glasses over ice, garnished with lemon slices and mint leaves.

Buttermilk Shake

SERVES 4-6

This low-fat beverage is a real thirst-quencher, and will be loved by kids and grown-ups alike, as long as you don't tell them it contains buttermilk until they've tried it. I first tried this drink after stooking peat in a peat bog, where temperatures soared over 100°F (50°C). It rejuvenates as well as refreshes, and it's a great conversation piece at a barbecue.

– R

1	banana, peeled and cut in chunks	1
2 Tbsp	frozen orange juice concentrate	30 ml
1/2 cup	fresh raspberries or strawberries	125 ml
1/3 cup	honey	75 ml
4 cups	cold buttermilk	1 l

In a blender or food processor, combine banana, juice concentrate, berries, and honey. Process briefly, and then pour in buttermilk while pulsing until smooth. Thin consistency, if desired, by processing with 1/4 cup (50 ml) crushed ice. Serve cold.

Strawberry Smoothie

SERVES 2

Smoothie bars are popping up everywhere these days. While treating the whole family can be expensive, smoothies are quite inexpensive when made at home. You can use almost any fruit or combination of fruits you like.

– R & W

2 cups	plain or strawberry yogurt	500 ml
1 cup	fresh or frozen strawberries	250 ml
1 cup	lemonade	250 ml
2 Tbsp	honey	30 ml
	sprig of mint, to garnish	

Combine smoothie ingredients in a blender, and process until smooth. Pour into two tall glasses, and garnish with mint.

Tangy Apple Cooler

SERVES 6-8

Coolers are very popular, with flavours becoming more exotic all the time. This tangy non-alcoholic cooler can be given a "kick" by adding vodka or white rum.

– R & W

3 cups	unsweetened apple juice, chilled	750 ml
2 cups	unsweetened pineapple juice, chilled	500 ml
1 cup	freshly squeezed orange juice, chilled	250 ml
2 Tbsp	freshly squeezed lemon or lime juice	30 ml
	orange, lemon, or lime slices, to garnish	

Combine juices in a large pitcher. Refrigerate for 1 hour, or until chilled. Serve in tall glasses over ice, garnished with citrus slices.

Cucumber Cooler

SERVES 2

This drink is an interesting blend of unexpected flavours. It is pretty to look at, and makes good use of a summer surplus of cukes. Sit back in a shady spot with a glass of this, and you'll really be as "cool as a cucumber."

– R & W

1 cup	unsweetened pineapple juice, chilled	250 ml
1 cup	peeled, seeded, and chopped cucumber	250 ml
1/2 cup	watercress	125 ml
1 tsp	chopped fresh parsley	5 ml
1/2 cup	finely crushed ice	125 ml
	cucumber slices, to garnish	

Combine all ingredients in a blender, and process until smooth. Pour into tall, ice-filled glasses, and garnish with a cucumber slice.

Strawberry Pound Cake Sundae

SERVES 8

Everyone will enjoy this easy, slightly decadent dessert. Buy a small pound cake at the bakery to keep things simple.

– R & W

1/2 cup	strawberry jam	125 ml
1 Tbsp	Amaretto or kirsch	15 ml
1	pound cake	1
4 Tbsp	melted unsalted butter	60 ml
1 pint	vanilla or strawberry ice cream	1/2 litre
1/2 cup	coarsely chopped toasted almonds	125 ml

Preheat barbecue to medium-low.

In a small pan, heat jam and liqueur over medium heat, stirring occasionally, until melted and smooth.

Cut cake into 1/2-inch (1-cm) thick slices. Brush both sides with melted butter. Place slices on oiled grill for 1-2 minutes per side, until golden brown. Place on individual plates, and add scoop of ice cream. Drizzle with 1 Tbsp (15 ml) warm jam sauce, and sprinkle with 1 Tbsp (15 ml) toasted almonds.

Banana Wham Bams

We first made this dessert on our television show. Ross insisted they were just for kids, until he watched in amazement as the staff and camera crew gobbled them up. Now we make them for our friends of all ages — and stand back!

– W

4	bananas, unpeeled	4
2 Tbsp	chocolate chips	30 ml
1/4 cup	peanut butter	50 ml
36	mini marshmallows	36

Preheat barbecue to medium.

Using a sharp knife, cut out a shallow wedge along the length of each unpeeled banana. Let the kids (or parents) nibble on these while they wait.

Press chocolate chips into banana flesh, and spread with peanut butter. Press marshmallows lightly into peanut butter and banana. Place bananas on grill, wedge-side up, and cook for 10-12 minutes or more, until marshmallows are melted and banana skins blackened. Remove from heat, using tongs and oven mitts. Let cool slightly, and then eat with spoon, directly from the peel.

Peaches Stuffed with Stilton

I can't get enough fresh peaches in the summertime. I've been known to eat five peaches cut up on my cereal, the cereal is obviously just an excuse to eat the peaches. This sweet and savoury recipe makes a wonderful starter or dessert.

— W

1/2 cup	crumbled Stilton	125 ml
4	peaches, peeled, pitted, and halved	4
1/4 cup	pecans or walnuts, chopped and toasted	50 ml

Preheat barbecue to hot.

Place peach halves on foil tray or pie plate. Fill cavities with cheese, and grill 1-2 minutes, until cheese is just melted. Sprinkle with toasted nuts, and serve hot.

Pecan Stuffed Apples

Choose a good baking apple for this recipe. Gravensteins are nice and tart, Melbas are sweet, and Paula Reds fall somewhere in between. In a pinch you can use Granny Smiths, but we prefer our local varieties.

– R & W

4	apples	4
1/4 cup	apple juice	50 ml
1 tsp	lemon zest	5 ml
1/3 cup	chopped pecans	75 ml
2 Tbsp	chopped dates	30 ml
	ice cream or whipped cream	
	pinch of cardamom	

Preheat barbecue to medium-hot.

Wash and dry apples. Core unpeeled apples about three-quarters of the way through. Place each apple on a square of double-thick aluminum foil.

In a small saucepan over medium-low heat, combine apple juice, lemon zest, pecans, and dates. Bring to a boil, stirring constantly. Simmer 2-3 minutes, until mixture begins to thicken. Cool slightly, and fill apples with mixture. Wrap foil around apples, and grill about 30 minutes, turning occasionally, until apples are tender. Serve warm, as is, or with ice cream or whipped cream sprinkled with cardamom.

Honey-Nut Grilled Apples

SERVES 4

These delicious baked apples can be made with honey or maple syrup. If you don't have either, substitute brown sugar. Our mothers used to make these in the oven as a special treat, and the barbecued version tastes every bit as good.

– R & W

4	apples	4
1/4 cup	raisins	50 ml
2 Tbsp	chopped walnuts or pecans	30 ml
1/4 cup	honey or maple syrup	50 ml
	butter	

Preheat barbecue to hot.

Core unpeeled apples about three-quarters of the way through. Place each apple on a square of aluminum foil. Press raisins and nuts into core cavities. Drizzle with honey or maple syrup, and dot each apple with butter. Wrap foil around apples, and bake for 15-20 minutes, until bubbling and fragrant. Unwrap carefully, and serve hot.

Maple Glazed Pineapple

Substitute brown sugar if maple syrup isn't available, stirring into butter until completely dissolved.

It's amazing how a tropical fruit such as pineapple goes so well with maple syrup. A scoop of ice cream makes it truly decadent!
– R & W

6	1-inch (2.5-cm) thick slices ripe, fresh pineapple	6
1/4 cup	butter	50 ml
1/2 cup	maple syrup	125 ml
1/4 tsp	dry ginger	1 ml
	non-stick cooking spray	

Preheat barbecue to medium-hot.

In a small saucepan, melt butter with maple syrup and ginger, stirring constantly until boiling. Keep warm on back of grill.

Spray grill lightly with non-stick spray. Lay pineapple slices on grill, and cook 3-4 minutes. Turn and brush slices with maple glaze, and grill for 3-4 minutes more. Turn again, brush with more glaze, and serve hot.

Reflector Oven Chocolate Cake

SERVES 6-8

As a member of the Yukon Voyageurs Canoe Club in Whitehorse in the early sixties, I made many extended canoe trips. Reflector oven cooking was as important to us as our tobacco or rum. After supper, when the campfire was still glowing with hot embers, out would come the reflector oven. We would choose between our homemade biscuit mix, cake, or pastry ingredients, and add any wild berries we'd found along the river that day.

Our reflector oven was fashioned from two aluminum baking sheets, connected on one side by a length of piano hinge. Two additional baking sheets had been salvaged and cut to create end caps for the reflecting sheets. A trough was riveted to both end caps to hold a rack that could support a pie plate, cake pan, or baking dish. Today, you can create your own reflector oven, or buy one from an outdoor or camping supply store. Carry an old leather glove to move or adjust the hot oven and lift out the hot pans.

— R

For the Cake:

1 1/2 cups	all-purpose flour	375 ml
1 cup	white sugar	250 ml
1/3 cup	cocoa	75 ml
1 tsp	salt	5 ml
1 tsp	baking soda	5 ml
1 tsp	baking powder	5 ml
1/3 cup	canola oil	75 ml

1 Tbsp	white vinegar	15 ml
1 tsp	vanilla	5 ml
1 cup	warm water	250 ml

For the Icing:

3 Tbsp	butter or margarine, softened	45 ml
2 cups	icing sugar	500 ml
3 Tbsp	cocoa	45 ml
	pinch of salt	
1/2 tsp	vanilla	2 ml
2 1/2 Tbsp	milk or water	40 ml

Build your fire against the face of a large rock outcropping to help reflect heat into the oven. Keep the fire small but hot, between 350°F and 400°F (180°C and 200°C); you should be able to hold your hand in front of the reflector oven for no more than 4 seconds. Have a supply of dry wood close by to keep the fire at a consistent heat.

Build a hot fire and get the reflector oven ready for use.

In a large bowl, combine dry ingredients. Add liquids, and mix well, until blended. Pour into greased 8-inch (20 cm) cake pan. Bake 35-45 minutes, rotating pan once or twice for even baking. Cake is done when it springs back to the touch. Allow to cool.

Meanwhile, in a small bowl, mix butter with icing sugar, cocoa, and salt. Add vanilla and water or milk, mixing until smooth and creamy. Spread on cooled cake.

Grilled Pears

This dessert is best made just before eating. Ripe Bosc pears hold their shape better than most, but you can use any variety.

– R & W

2	ripe pears	2
2 tsp	lemon juice	10 ml
2 Tbsp	melted butter	30 ml
1 Tbsp	brown sugar	15 ml
1/2 tsp	cinnamon	2 ml
1/4 tsp	ginger	1 ml
1/4 tsp	nutmeg	1 ml
	ice cream, to serve	

Preheat barbecue to low.

Peel pears, cut in half lengthwise, and remove core. Brush pears all over with lemon juice to prevent discoloration. In a small dish, combine butter, sugar, and spices. Brush pears with mixture, and place core-sides down on grill. Cook 2-3 minutes, turn, and spoon remaining sugar mixture into hollows. Grill 1-2 minutes more, and then remove from grill. Serve hot, with ice cream.

Index